"*Change Your Mind, Change Your Life* is a profound delivery of *The Seven-Point Mind-Training*. Jetsunma shares her own stories from more than fifty years as a Buddhist nun and of the wonderful nunnery she founded in the foothills of the Himalayas. Her years in the Dharma shine through each page and will truly bring transformation in the reader. This is a must-read for anyone who sincerely wants to practice the Dharma."

—LAMA TSULTRIM ALLIONE,
author of *Women of Wisdom* and founder of
Tara Mandala International Buddhist Community

"Reading and reflecting upon the teachings in this book is like sitting by a warm fire on a cold, dark winter night. In the midst of so much ignorance and confusion in our modern world, Jetsunma Tenzin Palmo's commentary on the aphorisms of Atisha are like a light that illuminates our minds, dispelling confusion and mistaken beliefs. Whether you are a beginner or a seasoned practitioner of the Buddha's teachings, this book can provide a framework for all the Dharma you practice in this lifetime, including your passage from this life to the next. It's a treasure."

—B. ALAN WALLACE,
author of *The Art of Transforming the Mind*

CHANGE YOUR MIND, CHANGE YOUR LIFE

The Transformative Power of Lojong Practice

JETSUNMA TENZIN PALMO

SHAMBHALA

Shambhala Publications, Inc.
2129 13th Street
Boulder, Colorado 80302
www.shambhala.com

Cover art: Dedraw Studio/Shutterstock
Cover design: Daniel Urban-Brown

9 8 7 6 5 4 3 2 1

First Edition
Printed in the United States of America

Shambhala Publications makes every effort
to print on acid-free, recycled paper.

Shambhala Publications is distributed worldwide
by Penguin Random House, Inc., and its subsidiaries.

LIBRARY OF CONGRESS CATALOGING-IN-PUBLICATION DATA
Names: Tenzin Palmo, 1943– author.
Title: Change your mind, change your life: the transformative power
of lojong practice / Jetsunma Tenzin Palmo.
Description: Boulder: Shambhala Publications, 2026 | Includes index. |
Identifiers: LCCN 2025029328 | ISBN 978-1-64547-439-5 (trade paperback)
Subjects: LCSH: Spiritual life—Bka'-gdams-pa (Sect) |
Ye-shes-rdo-rje, 'Chad-kha-ba, 1102–1176. Blo sbyong don bdun ma. |
Blo-sbyong. | Mind training (Buddhism)
Classification: LCC BQ7670.6 .T46 2026 | DDC 294.3/444—dc23/eng/20251119

LC record available at https://lccn.loc.gov/2025029328

The authorized representative in the EU for product safety
and compliance is eucomply OÜ, Pärnu mnt 139b-14, 11317 Tallinn, Estonia,
hello@eucompliancepartner.com.

CONTENTS

THE ROOT TEXT

The Aphorisms of The Seven-Point Mind-Training

Written down by Geshe Chekawa, from the lineage of Atisha

Translated by B. Alan Wallace

The First Point:
The Preliminaries

First, train in the preliminaries.

The Second Point:
Cultivating Ultimate and Relative Bodhichitta

Once you have achieved stability, reveal the mystery.
Regard phenomena as if they were dreams.
Examine the unborn nature of awareness.
Even the remedy itself is free right where it is.
Resting in the universal ground is the essential nature of the path.

Between sessions, be an illusory person.
Alternately practice giving and taking.
Mount them both upon your breath.
Three objects, three poisons, and three roots of virtue.
In everything you do, practice with words.
Begin the training sequence with yourself.

The Third Point:
Transforming Adversity into an Aid to Spiritual Awakening

When the whole world is enslaved by vices, transform adversities into the path of spiritual awakening.
Blame everything on one culprit.
Reflect on the kindness of everyone.
By meditating on delusive appearances as the four embodiments, emptiness becomes the best protection.
The best strategy is to have four practices.
Whatever you encounter, immediately apply it to meditation.

The Fourth Point:
A Synthesis of Practice for One Life

To synthesize the essence of this practical guidance, apply yourself to the five powers.
The Mahayana teaching on transferring consciousness is precisely these five powers, so your conduct is crucial.

The Fifth Point:
The Criterion of Proficiency in the Mind-Training

The whole of Dharma is synthesized in one aim.
Attend to the chief of two witnesses.
Constantly resort solely to a sense of well-being.

The Sixth Point:
The Pledges of the Mind-Training

Always abide by three principles.
Shift your priorities but stay as you are.
Do not speak of others' limitations.
Do not stand in judgment of others.
Whatever mental affliction is strongest, purify that first.
Abandon all hope of reward.
Avoid poisonous food.
Do not indulge in self-righteousness.
Do not engage in malicious sarcasm.
Do not wait in ambush.
Do not load the burden of a dzo on an ox.
Do not flatter your way to the top.
Avoid pretense.
Do not bring a god down to the level of a demon.
Do not take advantage of another's misfortune.

The Seventh Point:
The Precepts of the Mind-Training

Synthesize all meditative practices in one.
Respond in one way to all bouts of dejection.
There are two tasks, at the beginning and at the end.
Bear whichever of the two occurs.
Guard the two at the cost of your life.
Practice the three austerities.
Acquire the three principal causes.
Cultivate three things without letting them deteriorate.
Maintain three things inseparably.
Meditate constantly on the distinctive ones.
Do not depend on other factors.
Now practice what is important.
Make no mistake.
Do not be erratic.
Practice with total conviction.
Free yourself by means of investigation and analysis.
Do not try to make an impression.
Do not be bound by distemper.
Do not be temperamental.
Do not yearn for gratitude.

CHANGE YOUR MIND,
CHANGE YOUR LIFE

INTRODUCTION

This book is a commentary on an important text on *lojong*, or "mind-training," called *The Seven-Point Mind-Training*, which was composed by Geshe Chekawa Yeshe Dorje (1101–1176 C.E.). In my previous book, *The Heroic Heart*, I asked the question "Why is it so important to train and tame the mind?" That is, why is it imperative to release the mind from its habitual patterns and uncover its true nature? The answer in that book is quite simple, and it remains true: because a wild mind tends to harm others. At the heart of Buddhism is a passionate commitment to nonharm, loving-kindness, and compassion. There is nothing higher or greater in the Dharma than this. As I made clear in *The Heroic Heart*:

> From the simplest foundational practices to the heights of Mahamudra and Dzogchen, nothing is more important or higher than the selfless expression of boundless compassion, or *bodhichitta*. Training and taming the mind is the way we give rise to this boundless compassion, and the way we are ultimately able to express our true nature.*

---

* Jetsunma Tenzin Palmo, *The Heroic Heart: Awakening Unbound Compassion* (Shambhala Publications, 2022), 1.

Our true nature *is* our buddha nature. In reality we are not who or what we think we are. We are not our personalities or identities. Our true nature is vast, boundless, and ungraspable; our true expression is wise compassion and love. To reveal this mystery, to realize the truth of what we are, we need to tame the mind. One of the most powerful ways to do that is through the practice of lojong, a simple mindfulness practice that involves the repeated contemplation of certain aphorisms or slogans. My own master, the Eighth Khamtrul Rinpoche, greatly valued the lojong teachings. He considered them indispensable.

In Tashi Jong, a village in northern India, we have a group of monks who spend all their time in retreat. They are called *togdens*. If you have been to Tashi Jong, especially during any festivities, you probably noticed groups of men with dreadlocks wearing white skirts with the red and white striped *zens*. Although in the Tashi Jong Khampagar tradition togdens are monastics, they are also yogis. Most of them have spent all their life in retreat, since their teenage years or early twenties. Before the previous Khamtrul Rinpoche passed away, he said to them, "There's something I have to teach you. This is very important. I cannot leave here without teaching you this, so come tomorrow."

Of course, they were all speculating what it could be—obviously some really high, secret, super-deluxe Dzogchen transmission. The next day they all came together in great anticipation, and Rinpoche taught them this *Seven-Point Mind-Training*. He said, "This is the essence of the practice of the way. This is what you must master." So this is not just a text for beginners. This text is also for the masters of practice. It is for everyone who wishes to discover wisdom and compassion.

My lama, Khamtrul Rinpoche, was basically a quiet person.

He was very powerful, but he was also quiet. He didn't talk much at all. Apparently, when he was still in Tibet he hardly spoke. One time, before they were forced to flee Tibet, Dilgo Khyentse Rinpoche went to Khampagar to visit Khamtrul Rinpoche. Dilgo Khyentse's daughter, Chime Wangmo, told me the story. At that time, she was a little girl, and she and her father and mother went to Khampagar to visit the monastery. When they arrived and went to see Khamtrul Rinpoche, they sat down and were served tea, then everybody just sat there. After a while, Chime-la said to her mother, "What's the matter with this lama—can't he talk?" Her mother said, "Shush, he's a very high lama." So Chime said, "Well, Daddy's a high lama. He talks. What's the matter with this one?" So Khyentse Rinpoche had her taken outside. Khamtrul Rinpoche was a very quiet lama. On the other hand, I had heard that when he would spit outside his window, people would quickly gather up the spittle and put it in the sun, and it would dry into pearl-like *ringsel* (relics).

So on the whole Khamtrul Rinpoche didn't give much teaching. We learned from him mostly through his example. However, the one thing he would talk about, quite excitedly, was bodhichitta. As soon as he started talking on bodhichitta, it was like a torrent: He spoke very softly, but he would get breathless because he couldn't speak fast enough. He was so excited about bodhichitta, he would just light up.

So these teachings are very precious. Not the way I present them now, but the essential teachings. Please go and read books on lojong. There are many commentaries by great lamas available in English. We are blessed, because most of these commentaries by contemporary lamas, such as Dilgo Khyentse Rinpoche and His Holiness the Dalai Lama and others, are not available in Tibetan. Some commentaries on these lojong instructions approach them from a philosophical point of view, and others approach them from a practice-oriented or experiential point of view. Only the old commentaries are available in Tibetan; the modern commentaries are usually not. They were delivered and then translated, transcribed, and printed in Western languages. So we English readers are very privileged to have access to these wonderful commentaries by the great masters.

I do encourage you to read these commentaries, and then really think about them and apply them to your lives. I assure you, if we can really do this, it will transform our lives. As Geshe Chekawa says, if we practice the two bodhichittas—relative and ultimate bodhichitta—all our lives, perform our meditation properly, and mingle our minds with the view, our experience in daily life will not be ordinary.

The Seven-Point Mind-Training

The Seven-Point Mind-Training is one of the seminal works of lojong, and it is quite enigmatic. Unlike, for example, the *37 Practices of a Bodhisattva* by Thogme Zangpo, which has longer verses that give us a good idea of what the author intended, in *The Seven-Point Mind-Training* we are given seven points, and under each point there are a number of quite poetic slogans that are more figurative than literal. These slogans are like something you might put on a T-shirt and interpret however you feel. They could mean almost anything. This is why we need commentaries or teachings on this text: to interpret and apply the aphorisms correctly.

Over the years I have read several commentaries by teachers from the various traditions, and I have found various interpretations of the same slogans. Sometimes these commentaries seem to contradict each other. In the end, I followed the commentaries that made the most sense to me—in particular, those that focus on developing an experiential understanding through practice.

Although it does not contain many words, *The Seven-Point Mind-Training* is a very full text. Discussion of each short slogan could fill a whole book. Each aphorism unfolds to deeper and deeper levels of meaning when contemplated or applied in practice. In this book we are just going to skim the surface, so to speak, because the full meanings are so profound. This book is meant to provide you with a condensed and accessible explanation of what *The Seven-Point Mind-Training* is about. I advise you to read other commentaries as well.

Geshe Chekawa Yeshe Dorje

Geshe Chekawa Yeshe Dorje was born in central Tibet in 1101 C.E. This makes him a contemporary of Milarepa. In fact, for a time, Geshe Chekawa was a student of Rechungpa, who was the closest disciple of Milarepa. Chekawa Yeshe Dorje was born into a family that practiced in the Nyingma lineage of Tibetan Buddhism. When he reached adulthood he sought teachings from other lineages, as was the custom in Tibet, and this is how he met the lojong teachings. At the age of twenty Geshe Chekawa became a monk. At the age of thirty he heard *The Eight Verses of Mind-Training* by Langri Tangpa, which is well-known nowadays but was hardly known at all at that time, having been recently composed.

In the twelfth century these teachings on mind-training—on taking obstacles and using them as the path—were regarded as almost superhuman and so precious that they should be kept mostly secret. Therefore, they were given to only a few chosen people, not widely disseminated as they are now. Chekawa was deeply inspired by these lojong teachings. He had never heard of them before. *Give the victory to others. Accept defeat on yourself.* What? Who would say this? He had never heard anything like it. So he went to find a lama who was teaching these sorts of things.

Geshe Chekawa learned that we should take all harm and blame onto ourselves and give all gain and happiness to others. He was so intrigued by this unusual idea. Imagine if we could all do that in this world nowadays! Those who know even a little about the Buddhadharma might think, "Oh, we know. We take all the harm and blame ourselves and give all our gains to others." But how many in this world right now are truly able to do that? Bring it up at the United Nations and see what happens! When we have been in the Dharma for a while, we tend to take these revolutionary ideas for granted. But in this world, it is not the way most people are thinking. Even among Dharma followers, we may know the words, but how often do we practice it in our life?

Back to Geshe Chekawa: He traveled to Lhasa, in Central Tibet, in search of Langri Tangpa, who composed *The Eight Verses of Mind-Training,* only to discover he had already died. Then he came across Geshe Sharawa, who was teaching Shravakayana teachings—the teachings that focus on achieving liberation for oneself. Sharawa wasn't mentioning anything about bodhichitta—the mind of awakening that is infused with compassion for all beings and the determination to achieve enlightenment for the sake of others.

Geshe Chekawa said to Geshe Sharawa, "Langri Tangpa was giving these wonderful teachings on lojong, on mind-training.

How come you're not mentioning it?" Geshe Sharawa said, "Well, nobody is interested in that sort of thing. I can't talk about that; they wouldn't understand." Geshe Chekawa responded, "I will understand, please teach me." So Sharawa said, "If you stay with me for many years, I will teach you." And that is what Geshe Chekawa did. In time, Chekawa wrote this *Seven-Point Mind-Training* as the summation of his years of practice. He also founded a monastery called Cheka, but this text is his main legacy. Geshe Chekawa died in 1176 C.E., so he was seventy-five when he passed away.

Geshe Chekawa experienced a lot of ridicule, criticism, and difficulties in his life. This made him deeply grateful for this teaching that helps us to understand that what appear to be negative happenings in our life—criticism and blame and lack of appreciation and so forth—are great helpers on the path. Instead of resenting them, we should welcome them if they come and transform them into our Dharma practice. That is what this text is about. It provides seven points of practice that contain within them a number of slogans that we can use for training our mind to transform adversity into felicity and for cultivating a more loving, kind, and compassionate mind.

All the lojong, or mind-training, texts are part of the lineage or legacy of Atisha Dipankara (982–1054 C.E.). Atisha was a great Bengali scholar who traveled to Indonesia and stayed there for many years studying the lojong teachings, which he then brought back to the Indian subcontinent. Atisha was invited to Tibet, and although at first he refused because of his old age, his personal deity Arya Tara told him in a vision that it was very important for him to visit Tibet, even though it would shorten his life. So he went.

Of course, India was an ancient civilization, and Atisha, who was from a Brahmin family, was no doubt cultured and erudite. Tibet, on the other hand, was a scary place in those days. Although they had devotion, Tibetans were known for being rough and engaging in conflict and warfare. By that time the Dharma in Tibet, which had been degenerating since Guru Padmasambhava established it there in the eighth century, was almost decimated by the anti-Buddhist king Langdarma, who ruled between 841 and 842 C.E.

Atisha was particularly concerned that the foundational practices, such as holding the ethical precepts, had become overshadowed by rituals. He was also alarmed to discover that Tibetan monks and nuns were eating meat, which he saw as contrary to the Mahayana teachings. While he was in Tibet, Atisha tailored his Dharma teachings toward what seemed important for the Tibetans. He recognized that, at that time, of primary importance was not high philosophy or esoteric tantric practices, but developing true refuge, devotion, and bodhichitta. Therefore, Atisha's teachings emphasized these things, along with the mind-training of transforming difficulties into opportunities.

Atisha's teachings spread and they became a lineage known as Kadampa.* The original Kadampa was a precious lineage that was incorporated into all the Tibetan traditions. *The Seven-Point Mind-Training* by Geshe Chekawa is a crucial text within this Kadampa tradition. It was also the basis for Je Tsongkhapa's *Sunrays of Training the Mind* and many other lojong texts.

As noted earlier, Geshe Chekawa only uses maxims and aphorisms. There are no verses or longer descriptive passages

* Not to be confused with the New Kadampa Tradition.

in his text. He also uses a lot of colloquialisms from southern Tibet in the twelfth century, so it is quite difficult in the present day, even for scholars, to know what exactly he had in mind. The main points are taking obstacles onto the path of enlightenment through the cultivation of patience, taking suffering onto the path through equalizing and exchanging self and others, taking adverse conditions onto the path through turning one's adversaries into friends, and taking afflictions onto the path through the application of their relevant antidotes.

The lojong teachings tell us that difficult things we would normally regard as obstacles, as being adverse, become the path itself if we change our attitude. Therefore, if all is going well—the result of our good karma—that is wonderful; and if things are getting difficult, that is also wonderful, because now we can take those difficulties and transform them into opportunities for practice. The text returns to this point repeatedly: There is nothing that happens to us that cannot be used in the path. This is wonderful because, if we really understand it, then there is no hope and no fear. There's no hope that everything is going to go "right," or fear that it might go wrong (according to our ego's concepts). Everything can be accepted and made use of. This very profound understanding is the great contribution of the lojong teachings to the whole understanding of Tibetan Buddhism.

How to Use This Book

Nowadays in the West, many people equate Buddhism with formal sitting meditation, and practitioners complain that, with all their work and familial commitments, they have no time left over to practice. But of course, the Dharma involves a lot more than just formal sitting on a cushion.

These texts on lojong do not offer precise meditation instructions, nor are they intended to merely add to our intellectual understanding of Buddhist philosophy. Rather, they give us hints, which can be easily memorized, about how to skillfully cope with people and events in day-to-day life. As we read through the slogans, some may seem especially apt and helpful for dealing with our problems. We can take these to heart and repeat them to ourselves when faced with special challenges. They are a reminder that the Dharma is with us, at all times and under all conditions.

1

THE FIRST POINT

The Preliminaries

Geshe Chekawa's *The Seven-Point Mind-Training* starts right at the beginning, with the preliminaries. These preliminaries are: the precious human life, karma and rebirth, impermanence and death, and the unsatisfactory nature of samsara (the cycle of birth and death) as we experience it with our ordinary, conceptual minds. Everyone who has done the tantric preliminaries, or *ngondro*, knows that we first have to contemplate all these reflections in order to acknowledge our good circumstances and to get us motivated. They are commonly known as "the four thoughts that turn the mind to Dharma."

First, Train in the Preliminaries

The slogan for this point is simple: *First, train in the preliminaries.* These preliminaries are so important because they encourage us. So often, as we are going along our path, a problem comes up or something more exciting comes along, and then our path and practice get diluted. We lose interest; we lose inspiration. This means we need to develop a strong sense of purpose. Why are we bothering to practice? We have to remind ourselves again and again what it's all about, because whatever tradition we belong to, there is always the understanding that this is samsara: It is like a prison, and we are all trapped. We have to escape from the prison of samsara, either by leaving samsara behind or by transforming it: By recognizing that, from the very beginning, samsara and nirvana both refer to the mind, and if we understand things as they truly are, samsara transforms into nirvana. So there is actually nothing to escape from. However, as long as we are caught up in the prison house, simply saying that is just empty words. These preliminaries are to remind us that we are both imprisoned and that we have the opportunity to escape.

There are various ways one can practice with the four thoughts that turn the mind. It is possible to integrate the contemplations as part of a broader practice. For example, our nuns at Dongyu Gatsal Ling Nunnery recite some verses related to the preliminaries every morning before meditation, which helps them set a virtuous motivation for the practice. One can also sit with these contemplations individually and dive deeply into each of them, one by one. Again, the point of all of them is to remind us that our circumstances are incredibly unique and precious, so we must make good use of them while we can.

The Preciousness of Human Life

The first of the preliminaries is generating gratitude for having attained a precious human body and mind. Most readers probably know this already, but it is useful to be reminded. We need to start our Dharma practice immediately thinking, "Well, aren't we lucky we have this opportunity!" Even in the world today, we see so clearly that most people have no Dharma path. They may be very affluent and outwardly have everything, and yet inwardly they feel so empty because their life has no meaning beyond acquiring more and more. We all know this. Or perhaps they are born into a situation where they do not have the opportunity to practice Dharma. In many countries even today, there is no opportunity to study Dharma. Especially for women, the educational and the societal opportunities are not there, even in India.

Being educated means that we can pick up a book, read it, and understand it. I think many people don't recognize how rare that is. Even among our nuns, some may be able to read the words, but don't understand the meaning. This is why it is so important for nuns to get an education, because traditionally they did not receive one. With education we can pick up a book and, provided it is not about some arcane subject like quantum physics, have a good go at understanding what it is saying. That is an enormous advantage.

We can learn, and then we can think. We can hold two or three different views in our mind and think through them. The Buddha said that, first, we hear or read, then we go away and think about it. Do the things we learned make sense? What is the real meaning of it? What is the point? Then, if we agree, we can practice and incorporate it into our life.

A precious human birth basically means to have all the advantages and so forth, but the real point is that we have the freedom to find a spiritual path and practice it. Essentially, we must have a desire for the Dharma, because we can be in a Buddhist country, and have teachers who are talking in our language, and yet we have no interest. This is very common nowadays, as you know. Instead, there is an outer faith based on culture. People will say OM MANI PADME HUNG and do circumambulations, but any real interest in practicing and using the Dharma in daily life is simply not there. Nowadays genuine faith is quite rare.

So, when all these causes and conditions come together, don't waste your chance. These causes and conditions for meeting with the Dharma are something we ourselves created, in this and previous lifetimes. It is not an accident; the situation didn't arise out of nowhere. However, if in this lifetime we don't make good use of the opportunity to develop ourselves to the best of our abilities, next time around who knows where we will go? The chance to practice the Dharma may not come again. This is why the preciousness of human birth is the first and most important point. We mustn't waste this life and die with regrets.

Death and Impermanence

The second preliminary is contemplating on death and impermanence. Everything is changing from moment to moment, and we don't know how long we have left in this life. Just because we are young doesn't mean we aren't going to be dead tomorrow—especially on Indian roads. People who are still young and healthy and fit can have heart attacks; they can have accidents. Anything can happen—we just don't know. We cannot confidently say how long we're going to live. Maybe we will, maybe we won't. Everything is impermanent, but the one thing certain about life is death. That's the one thing we all have in common: Absolutely 100 percent of us are going to die.

Buddha said that, if we could do only one meditation, the meditation on impermanence and death should be it. This is not to make us miserable, but again to help us recognize how precious this human life is while we've got it. It is to remind us we are not going to live forever, so we had better practice now.

Karma and Rebirth

The third preliminary is karma and rebirth. You are, at this moment, about to read this text on lojong, and you are part of a minute section of society, out of all the beings in the world, who will read this. Somehow you have made the causes and conditions to read this Dharma text. This is considered to be the result of your past actions, or karma. You may think that you made the decision, but you were actually propelled by your own actions from past lives and also during this lifetime. All of it came together so that, at this particular point, you had the interest and opportunity to pick up this book and start reading.

So much of what happens to us, especially seminal things that happen to us, are the result of causes and conditions that we ourselves have created. How we respond to those situations creates more causes and conditions, as we constantly make our future. Moment to moment, we are eating up the past and creating the future. It is all unfolding continuously.

Much of what happens in our lives is not arbitrary, not just coincidence, but a part of our individual patterning that we are experiencing at this time. Therefore, it is very important that whatever happens to us—this again is part of the lojong—we don't judge it as good or bad. What we need to think is this: "How can I respond to this situation with compassion and intelligence, in a way that opens up future opportunities?" Much of what happens to us is good or bad only according to our narrow, egoic ideas. So often, things that we think are unfortunate turn out to be the best thing that could happen. Likewise, things that we think are great don't necessarily lead to much. Therefore, we shouldn't judge things by whether they are comfortable or uncomfortable for our ego; instead, we should ask ourselves: "What can I learn from this? What is this going to teach me?"

The Suffering of Samsara

The fourth of the preliminaries is the difficult state of samsara. No matter whether it looks like a god realm or a hell realm that we are living in, it is still part of the prison. We are still entrapped. We are entrapped not by our external circumstances but by our own internal delusion and ego grasping. And, as long as we retain this fundamental ignorance of the way things really are, we are going to suffer. We suffer because everything is impermanent, yet we want it to be secure and stable. We just don't know what is going to happen, when it is going to happen, how it is going to happen, and yet our ego wants everything to be safe and settled and going the way the ego thinks things should be going. The ego equals ignorance, so why are we endlessly following ignorance?

Again and again, the Dharma is trying to help us to break out, even for an instant, to see things as they really are, and not as our ordinary, deluded, conceptual mind thinks they are.

2

THE SECOND POINT

Cultivating Ultimate and Relative Bodhichitta

Geshe Chekawa's second point of mind-training is *the cultivation of bodhichitta.* The first thing we need to understand about bodhichitta is that there are two kinds: ultimate bodhichitta and relative bodhichitta. Relative bodhichitta is the aspiration to attain enlightenment for the benefit of all beings. This is important, very fundamental: Why are we bothering to practice? Is it just to make ourselves feel better? To flatter and soothe our self? To make samsara feel more comfortable? Or is it because, having seen the way things are in the prison of samsara, our heart opens with great compassion for all beings, recognizing how we are all included in this dilemma? Recognizing how much we are interconnected at a deep level is relative bodhichitta. It is conditioned bodhichitta. We will discuss relative bodhichitta more later.

In practical terms, the first step after the preliminaries is to cultivate an understanding of ultimate bodhichitta, and this is what Geshe Chekawa presents next.

Ultimate Bodhichitta

Ultimate bodhichitta is basically buddha nature. When we talk about buddha nature, we say that we all have buddha nature. Every sentient being, meaning every conscious being, has buddha nature—in fact, *is* buddha nature. We are all buddhas. Even ants and mosquitoes have buddha nature, not just humans. Now, one problem with saying we have buddha nature is that we might envision a nice little Buddha sitting inside each of us—my buddha nature versus your buddha nature. We might think, "Well, actually, my buddha nature is really rather special." It is very important not to think like that. It is not an inflated sense of self—a bigger, better, more wonderful "Me," all beautiful and radiating light.

In order to refute that idea, buddha nature—which is also synonymous with the nature of the mind—is compared to space. We will go into this later. For now we just need to understand that, just like space, the nature of mind cannot be grasped. We cannot see it, we cannot quantify it, and yet it is all pervading. Space is everywhere. Even solid objects, such as tables and chairs, are nothing more than space. Even our bodies are space. Everything is space. Buddha nature is not something we can grasp and say, "This is mine." It is the opposite of that. Geshe Chekawa starts by encouraging us to work toward this quality of the mind—our pure, primordial awareness, both lucid and empty—beyond the subject and object dichotomy. The nature of the mind is beyond duality; it is the pure knowing *before* the split into knower and known.

Once You Have Achieved Stability, Reveal the Mystery

The first slogan under point two says, *Once you have achieved stability, reveal the mystery*. Gaining stability refers to the practice of *shamatha* or calm abiding meditation. If you were a surgeon about to perform an operation, the first thing you would need to do is to get the tools precisely in good condition: Your scalpel has to be sharp, and it has to be clean. This is what we have to do with the mind. We are going to do a delicate operation on the mind. We are going to analyze the mind itself—that which is beyond our ordinary, conceptual consciousness. For that, we need to get the mind in good working order. And to achieve that, we start with shamatha.

Shamatha—Calm Abiding

The point with any shamatha practice is that we're trying to cultivate awareness. We are trying to transform our current state of mind—which the Buddha himself compared to a mad monkey—into a mind that is workable and usable. To do this we use different tools, such as the breath, a visualized image, bodily sensations—whatever is most suitable for the individual; it doesn't really matter. Ultimately, what we're trying to do is to become more aware and make the mind one-pointed.

As the mind becomes calm and clear, we are able to consciously and intentionally direct it, to place our attention on the object without distraction. This is the foundation for all meditation practice. It sounds very simple, but that doesn't mean it's easy. Just like everything else, it requires practice. However, we need to do this in a relaxed manner; there is no use in pushing ourselves to be more aware. We need to practice and make diligent efforts, but at the same time we need to relax.

Calm abiding meditation by itself does not lead to enlightenment, but it does create the right conditions for the mind to be most useful for the path. While our monkey minds are distracted, our attention span is short—it's said to be four seconds at the most—and we are full of the inner noise of our background thinking. We cannot stay focused on anything for long. We cannot use that kind of mental state to probe the nature of the mind; it is just not workable.

In the early sutras of the Pali canon, the Buddha put a lot of emphasis on attaining what are called the *jhanas*, the various levels of mental absorption. Before attaining enlightenment, the Buddha himself practiced both the form and the formless jhanas. He recognized that they did not in themselves lead to liberation, but he did not abandon these states of concentrated absorption, because he recognized that they make the mind supple, clear, and sharp. So when we come to doing *vipashyana* or insight meditation, our mind is a precise and helpful tool instead of an obstacle, thanks to practicing the jhanas.

Nowadays, due to the influence of nineteenth- and twentieth-century Burmese Buddhist masters, there is a lot of emphasis on vipashyana and not so much on shamatha, especially in the West. Some people even believe that shamatha is a waste of time. The result is that many people who have been practicing vipashyana for years and who do gain insights while on retreat find that when they leave the retreat situation, all those insights evaporate. They find themselves back where they started. Rather than realizing that their foundation must be built with shamatha first, some of these people think that meditation doesn't work, or even maybe the Buddha was wrong. There is a lot of questioning right now about why people who have been practicing for twenty or even forty years are not enlightened yet. Perhaps it is because the foundation was not firmly laid in these deep levels of shamatha meditation, where the mind is completely at one with its object.

If we consistently practice shamatha meditation, after a while the meditation seems to leave the brain center and goes down into the center of our being. We can feel a definite shift. At that point the subject of meditation and the object of meditation completely merge. When that happens, then the practice becomes truly transformative; and there are stable, observable results.

I think this is a very important point. For example, consider the togdens, the yogi monks of Tashi Jong I mentioned in the introduction. Some years ago, because it was the three-hundredth anniversary of the Khampagar lineage, many of the togdens came out of retreat. These were retreatants who hadn't been seen in public for fifteen or twenty years. The reason why they are not usually on display, and why they are in retreat for such long periods, is that their practice needs to be fully accomplished before they come out. The analogy I give is baking a cake. We gather and mix all the ingredients together and put the mixture in a hot oven. We leave the cake to cook. The cake will soon start to rise. If we take out the cake just then, though, when it is not cooked through, it will collapse and be yucky. A half-baked cake is disgusting. But if we leave the cake in the oven until it cooks all the way through, then when we take it out, not only will it not collapse but it will keep its shape and be nourishing and delicious. That is the point. The togdens are not taken out of their yogic oven until they are fully cooked. This is why some of them have white lower robes, whereas others wear the burgundy robes of a monastic, even though some practitioners have the dreadlocks. The ones in white are "fully cooked." They have stable realization of the true nature of mind.* Four of our nuns were recently recognized as *togdenmas* after sixteen years of dedicated retreat.

An important aspect of achieving that stable realization is the foundational practices. For the first few years, the togdens and togdenmas practice shamatha and cultivate bodhichitta. This is because we first need to get a firm foundation in taming the mind, training the mind to be settled and sharp and clear, while at the same time arousing the bodhichitta motivation so that the path doesn't become self-centered and self-cherishing. This is very important.

In the text from Geshe Chekawa, this part of the journey is covered in just three words, but it might take years. The first line just says, "having gained stability." It might take us years and years to get the mind to a level where, when we wish it to be focused on a certain point, it will settle there—clear, bright, and completely merged with the object of meditation. This book is not about shamatha meditation, so I won't go into more detail except to say that those three words of Geshe Chekawa probably cover years and years of meditation practice.

The other reason we need to gain stability is that, if we are in any way mentally or emotionally unbalanced, we cannot practice further levels of the path. First, we have to heal the mind.

* The wearing of white robes by monastics to indicate their realization of the true nature of mind is unique to the Khampagar tradition. In other traditions, wearing white can indicate that the person holds the five Buddhist precepts or the Upasaka or Upasika vows, or simply that they belong to a nonmonastic lineage.

It is very important that we deal with this. We need to make the mind healthy, balanced, and able to practice further. If we try to take on too much too soon, it is not going to work. Then we will become disheartened either with ourselves or with the technique.

Shamatha is a very healing meditation. We cannot go into deeper states of meditation if the mind is not in balance. This is why the Buddha placed it first. We have to make our minds healthy and serviceable. Then, when we have that wonderful tool of our own mind working for us on the conventional level, we can make use of it to go beyond. If we are mentally unbalanced, we have to put our own house in order on this mundane level before probing the depths of ultimate reality. But we shouldn't be in too much of a hurry; more haste leads to less speed.

We have to get our conventional mind in good shape before going to the unconditioned. Otherwise, even if we get flashes of insight into the true nature of things, it is not going to stabilize. The insight is not going to last. And it might end up just inflating the ego. We can tell when our spiritual path is working when the ego begins to evaporate a little bit, our absorption with ourselves begins to lessen, and our sense of empathy with others begins to increase. If we get more and more absorbed in ourselves, then we are probably not on the right path; it is not working.

"Revealing the mystery" is another way of saying that we settle the mind in its natural state, perhaps by using our breath or another object; we have stabilized our attention. However, the mind is still chattering away in the background—the inner television is still on—but we are reading an interesting text, and we are not paying attention to the noise in the background.

In terms of meditation, maybe the chatter continues in the background, but the focus of our awareness is on the object of our meditation, whatever it is. The mind settles there. It is not wandering off every two seconds. It has become quieter and settled on the object of concentration. The background noise is muted; the volume is turned down and we are not listening anymore. At that point, we can turn the focus of our concentration onto the mind itself. We just sit and look at the mind.

This chattering mind in itself is interesting. Normally, when we are thinking, either we are carried away by our thoughts or we are caught up in the input coming through the sense doors. What we are seeing, what we are hearing, what we are smelling—the mind goes out and grasps those sense experiences. This is why shopping malls are so popular, at least in many parts of Asia. On their days off, people take the whole family to shopping malls, and they spend all their time eating and gazing into shop windows, and all the attention is going outward. Alternatively, if our interest is not occupied by our sense doors, then we are caught up in our memories and dreams, our fantasies, plans, ideas, opinions, and judgments. We are engulfed in all this mental activity and swept along by it.

Now, having trained the mind a little bit to stay focused—this mindfulness is a quality of observing—instead of being caught up in the object, we can step back and observe it—without judgment, without opinions, just seeing things as they are, without interfering. To start, we are developing this mindfulness first on the breath or on some other object or, if one is doing visualizations, then maybe by visualizing the Buddha. Finally, we take that awareness, that beam of attention, and we turn it inward onto the mind itself. We watch this conceptual mind, which is running along all the time with images, thoughts, feelings, ideas, memories, plans, endless chatter. Now we look at it. We just sit back and observe.

This is still shamatha, observing the flow of the thoughts, and as we observe this flow, we notice there is a space. We are not *in* the thoughts anymore. We become able to recognize that there is another aspect of the mind that is capable of observing the thoughts. All of us can do this. We don't have to be submerged in the stream; we can sit on the bank. This in itself is a great relief, because we begin to see how the mind itself is constantly changing, from moment to moment. It is like a movie. The little frames are going so fast that they are creating this projection, but it is just a movie.

As we develop the ability to focus on the mind itself, then the mind naturally begins to slow down. As our concentration becomes stronger, the stream of thoughts becomes slower. It can happen that sometimes the whole thing falls apart and we actually can observe the gap between the past thought and the future thought. There is a distinct gap. In that gap, if we are watching, then we see what is behind that running film, which is in fact the nature of the mind.

In the metro stations of the London Underground, a recorded voice says, "Mind the gap," as each train comes to a stop. This is because there's a gap between the platform and the train carriage. The whole point of this kind of meditation is to mind the gap between thoughts, so many meditators have taken this as their slogan. *Mind the gap.* Once we recognize the gap, the practice is to make more frequent gaps and to extend their duration.

This is called resting in the nature of the mind. It is still shamatha meditation, and it has evolved from stabilizing or calming the mind to getting to know our conceptual mind. This is how we recognize that there is something beyond our conceptual thinking. The conceptual mind is all these thoughts racing along, streaming along, but since we can observe them, we now *know* that we are not the thoughts. The fact that we can step back and look at them proves that they are not who we are.

This is the first step in recognizing that we should not identify so closely with our conceptual thinking. The problem is, when we think something, we tend to believe it is true, and then we identify with it. We believe our memories, ideas, and opinions. This is very dangerous. In the world today, people are killing each other all the time, all based on their beliefs, which are just thoughts. All ideologies are based on thinking, rooted in this deluded conceptual mind, that is permeated with greed and aggression, jealousy and pride, with an underlying total ignorance of the way things really are. All our actions and words depend on our mind—which is frightening, because our mind is usually a total mess.

Probably the most common thing people discover when they first start meditating is the chaos their mind is in and that they live in that mess. They thought they were nice, sane, normal human beings, but now they see that is just on the surface. If we were living in a house full of trash and muck, we would need to clear it out by deciding what is useful and what is not useful. That is exactly what we need to do with our mind.

Not that there's anything wrong with thinking. The mind itself is wonderful. There's nothing wrong with having feelings either. Otherwise, we would be a log of wood, a corpse. The lojong teachings are not against conceptual thought, which can be an incredible tool. In fact, our particular kind of human intellect is what makes us capable of practice. Thoughts are not the problem. The problem is that we totally *identify* ourselves with our thoughts and are even *controlled* by them. Most of our thoughts are a manifestation of the ignorance of our minds; that is all. We have to understand how the mind works, and the first step is cultivating the ability to observe the mind. Once we learn how to observe the mind, which is still shamatha, then we can go onto vipashyana.

Vipashyana—Insight into the Nature of the Mind

Once we have gained stability in our shamatha practice, we turn that clear awareness to the mind itself. What we are trying to do at this stage is recognize the true nature of the mind, and we can do that by paying close attention and investigating something that is constantly being produced by the mind: thoughts.

Here, vipashyana means starting to question the mind. We start to question our thoughts. What is a thought? What color is it? What does it look like? Where does it come from? Where does it go? Where does it stay? When we get sensory input from the outside, how does our mind deal with this basic data from our senses?

There's a whole slew of questions to be asked about thoughts and feelings and their real nature. When we analyze like that, which takes quite some time, we begin to see that the problem with thinking is that it makes everything seem so solid and real. Our ideas about ourselves and our ideas about everything outside of ourselves—other people and objects and things that happened to us—all seem so real. Our thinking mind reifies everything in our experience. In other words, it makes it into a "thing," something solid and immutable and definitely existing on its own. This is our commonsense way of understanding things.

We believe that, if we were to die, everything else would remain as it appears to us now. We believe that, from our side, we are not really adding anything to what we perceive. We are merely neutral, just noting what actually exists outside of ourselves, just how it appears to us. Normally we don't understand how much we contribute to our version of reality. There are a few ways we can deal with that. We can go the way of science, such as quantum physics and neuroscience, and try to understand these things from a scientific point of view. Alternatively, we can go the way of Buddhist practice. From the practice point of view, we start to understand reality from the inside out—which isn't the way it appears to the deluded, samsaric mind—and to recognize how much we actually are contributing to our version of what appears to be.

When we start to look at thoughts and feelings and start to analyze them, we begin to see that our ideas and emotions, and our view of ourselves, are not something solid, static, and tangible. In fact, the more we analyze the mind, the more it keeps disappearing. It is like trying to look at a rainbow. A rainbow looks very solid, but when we go toward it we can never reach it; it keeps receding. Likewise with our thoughts and our feelings: When we start to analyze them, we can't catch hold of them; they are not solid at all. In some ways they are like bubbles, bright and shiny, but with a snap of the fingers there is nothing there. This is one of the meanings of *shunyata,* or emptiness, in Buddhist terminology.

When Geshe Chekawa says "reveal the mystery," he is referring to this empty nature. Empty doesn't mean it doesn't exist.

Empty doesn't mean nothing; that would be nihilism. The idea that things exist solidly, immutably, from their own side, or just how they appear would be one extreme; and the other extreme is that they don't really exist at all. Buddhism teaches the middle way, between extremes. What this means when we are talking about emptiness—shunyata—is that our thoughts and feelings are not something solid, real, and self-existent. Each one that comes into being is conditioned by what went before it, and it conditions what will come after it. They are all interconnected and preconditioned.

If we look for a thought, we can never catch it; we can never find it. This is why looking at the mind is so important, because by observing the mind we begin to realize thoughts are just like impulses of energy in the mind stream; they are not real of themselves. Our problem is not the thoughts. We can use them—they are very useful—but they are not who we really are. Our problem is that we believe our thoughts and identify with our thoughts. We think, "This is who I am."

Therefore, this meditation of looking at the thoughts and seeing how they rise and whir around is important because then we recognize that we cannot possibly *be* those thoughts. After all, the minute we think we are a particular thought, another thought comes along. Yes, there is water, but the river is changing from moment to moment. The sense that there is nothing solid, real, and immutable when it comes to thoughts is what is meant by the "empty nature" of the thoughts. It is obvious if we think about it. Therefore, shunyata, this empty quality, is what is called the mystery. So "reveal the mystery" means that, once we have achieved stability in our meditation, when we look at the mind and we look at the flow of our thoughts and emotions, that will show us the empty, luminous nature of the mind. That is the mystery, the secret.

The most important thing we can do in this life is to recognize the nature of the mind. Beyond that, nothing else really matters. But the important point is—and Geshe Chekawa's text will go through this—a mere glimpse of reality is not enough. As I say about our togdens and togdenmas in training, *togpa* means the realization of the nature of the mind, and *den* means to have it. Therefore, they wear ordinary robes until their realization of the nature of mind is considered to be stable—until their cake is baked all the way through, more or less. Then they are given the white robes and the striped shawl. Until then, they are not called togdens or togdenmas.

We now have a number of nuns in our long-term retreat center. Four of them have just been given their white lower robes and striped zens after completing sixteen years of retreat. All the retreat nuns have the aspiration to become togdenmas, so please say some prayers for them that they can do this. They are totally devoted, and the togdens are taking them seriously. Many high lamas have visited the retreat center to see them and talk with them. They often speak with these nuns for one or two hours, then talk with each nun separately. This is very good for the nuns, to see that the lamas are taking their aspirations seriously. We hope in the future that some of them will become teachers, because we also need more female teachers, as we all know.

With realization, the first breakthrough is the most important. In the early schools, it was called "entering the stream." In Zen, it's called *kensho* or *satori*. It is that first breakthrough into recognizing the nature of the mind, but it is just the beginning. My lama, Khamtrul Rinpoche, said that, when we recognize the nature of the mind, then we start to meditate. All the rest is preparation. From the point of recognition onward, we know clearly what we are trying to do. The whole point is to gradually widen the gap until finally we are in a state of primordial awareness twenty-four hours a day, or we can be in that state the moment we want to be.

For this to be possible, we need to have all this preparation that creates a firm foundation on which to build up the practices. If the mind is not ready, then when that person gets a glimpse—sometimes people get powerful flashes of insight, especially when they are not expecting it—they might think they are enlightened. They might set themself up as a guru. That is very dangerous, dangerous for everybody.

Even on a Dzogchen path, the most advanced or "highest" of the Buddhist practice traditions, there is still a focus on preparing the mind. However, in Dzogchen they usually start with recognition of the nature of the mind, then they go back to the beginning. They also do shamatha and vipashyana, because we have to get the mind in good working order to understand the mind. Then everything goes smoothly.

If we are driving a car and there is something wrong—say the brakes are not working or fuel is all messed up and dirty—then the car is going to break down. It is not going to work. If we want to go on a long journey, we have got to cover the basics and get our vehicle in good working order. It is not exciting, but it is important not to skip stages. Each level builds on and enhances the other.

Most of the commentaries on Geshe Chekawa's *The Seven-Point Mind-Training* make it clear that, before receiving the secret teachings on ultimate bodhichitta—the ultimate nature of the mind, which is emptiness and lucidity—we must stabilize the mind through meditation. We must also gain full conviction and understanding of the basics, such as the preciousness of our human life, the truth of impermanence, and the suffering of samsara.

As long as our minds remain untamed, we should not think that we are in a fit psychological state to attempt higher practices. This is because if the mind has distortions, then everything we do will be distorted. The first thing we need to do is to attain psychological balance. The Buddha himself always stressed that before doing practices—any practices, including insight meditation and so on—we should first stabilize the mind with shamatha meditation, with calm abiding. This is because, in order to attain genuine calm abiding, all the psychic faculties have to be in balance. Only then will the mind become calm, centered, and focused. That kind of mind, not only calm but also peaceful and centered, is also what Tibetans call *lesu-rungwa*. It is *workable* and flexible. We can use it.

It is like a potter with a heavy piece of clay: First he must knead it and twist it until it is soft and pliable enough to be used, so that it is workable. This is very important. Nowadays everybody is in such a hurry, they always want to get immediately to the highest yoga tantras or Dzogchen or Mahamudra. Everyone wants to do that. They are thinking, "Look, it says in the text: That method is the best! I want that. I only want the best. And it also says it is a quick one—enlightenment in one lifetime. Right, that's what I'm going for."

It is like we are saying, "Okay, I want to play a Beethoven concerto because that is the very best." But if we don't even know the scales, then what? We all understand this regarding mundane activities—that we have to start with simple things, such as musical scales, and go over them again and again so we can master them. We say that practice makes perfect. This is an important point.

Nowadays some teachers go around saying, "You should do my practice because it is effortless, and you shouldn't make any effort." But it actually takes a lot of effort to become effortless. We also know this. We know this in sports, in art, in music. We see these great musicians playing, and the music flows through them, so seemingly effortless, but that happens only after thousands of hours they spent practicing. They worked at it until they could drop their ego and allow the music to play through them. So, if that is so for our fingers, what about our minds? Our minds are especially tricky. We have been in samsara for a long time, and we have become habituated to a lot of bad habits. To rework the mind, to learn how to drop the bad habits and develop some good habits, takes a lot of effort.

At Dongyu Gatsal Ling, our nunnery near the Tashi Jong community in northern India, we built a temple. It is a small temple by many standards, but it is elaborately decorated. When people visit, they see the beautiful murals and the golden roof, but no one thinks about the pit we had to dig to lay a strong basis, to place the foundation and all the plumbing. Before we could build the walls, before we could paint the murals on the walls, and certainly before we got the golden roof, we had to lay a deep foundation. This is invisible, and no one thinks about it when they visit; yet without that foundation, the whole building would collapse.

When we were building, no one said, "Oh, come look at this beautiful foundation—it is fantastic! Look at that sewage system—wow! The best in northern India!" It cost us a fortune and months of work, but nobody cares about sewage and foundations. Yet without them, the rest cannot be built. It is the same for our minds. A lot of these practices are not romantic, and they don't sound very exciting, but we must do the basic groundwork so that we get really solid, strong foundations for transforming our mind. Then all the rest comes easily.

Sometimes people do all these fancy meditations for years and years, but has the mind transformed? It is not how many millions of mantras we say, how many hundreds of thousands of prostrations we do. The point is, how do we practice and with what motivation? How are we dealing with situations that happen to us moment to moment, day after day? This is the point. Our fundamental state of mind, what are we doing with it?

Atisha himself said that even if we spend a year in retreat and get wonderful experiences and realizations, at the end of that retreat the question we need to ask is: "Have my negative afflictive emotions—my greed and grasping, my irritation and anger, my pride, my jealousy, and my basic sense of 'me'—have they decreased, increased, or stayed the same?" Obviously, if they have increased, if we are more irritable, more egocentric and proud because "Now I have done a year of retreat, so I am something special; I can call myself a lama," or if our afflictive emotions have stayed the same, then that retreat was a waste of time, says Atisha. The only true indication of whether the practice is working is whether our afflictive emotions have decreased. This is something important. At the end of the day, are we nicer people? *That* is the question. Are we more spontaneously kind, generous, thoughtful, and considerate or not? This is what Geshe Chekawa is referring to when he says "having gained stability."

Stability means that the mind becomes more settled and clearer, more focused and aware, and not so tossed around by the tumultuous waves of samsara.

Samsara is likened to an ocean because oceans have waves. Waves go up, waves go down. The Buddha compared the Dharma to a boat. A boat rides on the waves of samsara. It is not engulfed in the waves of samsara, but it also doesn't transform the ocean. The ocean still has waves going up and down, but we are no longer immersed; we ride the waves. Achieving that kind of stability is important before the secret is finally revealed. So Geshe Chekawa starts at the top. If we can get that level of stability, then we can stop reading here. For those who don't get it, then you have to keep reading.

Having established a foundation of mental balance also means having an inner sense of contentment that is stable no matter what happens. We misunderstand happiness by thinking that it is an abundance of pleasure. The world generally thinks like, "If we keep having more and more pleasures, we will stay happy." But we know that this is not true. This is not what the Buddha meant when he spoke of happiness. Happiness is an inner resource, a spring of inner well-being and joy inside ourselves. Like spring water bubbling up from the earth, it is clear, translucent, delicious, and refreshing. When our mind is mentally stable, we feel that inner joy.

Recognizing Mental Afflictions and Dealing with Them

It is not that we attain mental balance then immediately become perfect. It is not that we suddenly become free of greed, anger, jealousy, or any of the other afflictions, but we do have the inner poise to recognize these afflictions as they arise and to deal with them intelligently and skillfully. The ability of mind for becoming centered is developed, so whatever does come into our mind, we can deal with it skillfully. We are not completely thrown around by our emotions. It doesn't mean that we are high-level bodhisattvas, but at this point we can look at our emotions, recognize them, and then say, "Okay, this is the antidote to that emotion," and apply it.

Then we have a genuine sense of refuge and trust in the Dharma. This is important. The Three Jewels really and truly are the refuge, if one is a Buddhist. Even if one is not a Buddhist, still the Dharma can be understood as revealing the way things truly are, which is not how we usually imagine that they are—this is our genuine refuge. We take refuge in our true nature, which is not how we usually think we are. That is the ultimate refuge for us: to see things as they truly are.

Geshe Chekawa acknowledges that exploring the nature of ourselves and the world around us can be a terrifying experience. One of the outcomes of this exploration is the experience of shunyata, or emptiness, which is not a trivial matter. Shunyata is often referred to as a mystery or a secret. When he says, "having gained stability, reveal the mystery," he is referring to the ultimate emptiness of ourselves and everything around us. Shunyata is considered a mystery or secret because it cannot be known through our senses. This experience can have a profound effect on the mind, radically transforming it.

I am not a *geshema* or a *khenmo*—a person with the equivalent of a PhD in Buddhist studies. I have never studied philosophy, and what understanding I have comes from my own reading and reflection and practice rather than formal study.

People spend twenty years trying to understand shunyata, so my ability to express shunyata in words is somewhat elementary. However, the basic truth of shunyata is that things are not the way that they appear to be. Our mind naturally reifies everything.

To reify means to make something abstract into something concrete or solid. That is, we are always making things into *things*. And that starts with ourselves. If we have read any Buddhist philosophy, we know that the self is not solid or independently existing. Yet we still believe that we are somehow an unchanging entity that inherently exists: "I am *me*, and that makes me different from all the *yous*."

When the Buddha talked about *anatma*, no-self, what he was refuting was this underlying, unquestioned idea of who we are. We believe that somehow, from since we were born up until the present, there has been this solid, immutable, unchanging *me* basically at the center of the universe, and everything else spins around me. So the Buddha said, "Okay then, find it! Look for this 'I.' Where is it?" A lot of Buddhist meditation is dealing with the search for this otherwise unquestioned sense of a self at the center of our being.

Analytical meditations start out quite gross, or concrete: Okay, where is the "I"? Is it in the head? Is it in the foot? Is it at the heart? What does it look like? What color is it? What size is it? Where does it go when we are asleep? Gradually the probing becomes more subtle, looking into our consciousness to locate this "I" that we predicate and that seems to be at the center of our existence.

The Buddha said that this sense of "I" is our inherent ignorance. In Buddhism there are three main poisons: ignorance, attachment, and aversion. Ignorance doesn't mean not knowing about quantum physics. It means not seeing things as they really are. The most deeply ingrained version of that is our very strong sense of self, which arises even in young children—a strong sense of ego that we carry along with us lifetime after lifetime, even though, if we could meet ourselves in our last lifetime, we would not recognize ourselves. People who can recall their past lives have this sense of "I," even though their personas are different. They might be a different gender, a different nationality, yet at that moment there is still that strong sense of ego at the center.

There is the emptiness of external phenomena, and there is also an inner emptiness that dissolves our sense of ego. When we say that the ego is empty, this means that it is ungraspable. We cannot find it. Meanwhile, our "I"-ness goes a long way with us. Perhaps we have to appreciate this. Ultimately, we are not who we think we are; nonetheless, without a deep experience of the nature of the mind, this sense of "I" will accompany us for a long time. Most of this text and much of the Buddhadharma deals with how to cope with our relative sense of ego, in other words, how to navigate life skillfully while we are still holding on to this strong sense of self.

According to the Theravada system, we only completely drop this sense of "I" at the time of realizing nirvana. Only an *arhat* lives in the world egolessly. From the Mahayana point of view, maybe only bodhisattvas on the eighth spiritual level gain a really decisive realization—not just a glimpse, but a totally transformative experience of egolessness. After that, as bodhisattvas, they are no longer ruled by the sense of a personal ego.

What it means is that for the rest of us, for most of our spiritual lives—until we get arhatship or become eighth-level bodhisattvas—we have to take our ego with us. That is the bad news. However, the Chittamatra, or Yogacharya, system of Buddhist philosophy that was founded by the masters Asanga and Vasubandhu posits that there are eight consciousnesses: There are the five sense consciousnesses—eyes, ears, nose, taste, touch—and the sixth that is mental consciousness. Then there is the eighth consciousness, called the *alaya vijnana* in Sanskrit, that means "storehouse consciousness." We will discuss the seventh in a moment.

Chekawa's text also deals with storehouse consciousness to a degree. In Tibetan, it is called *kunzhi,* meaning the basis of everything—the all-basis—which some scholars translate as the "substrate consciousness." It is the ground in which all our memories are buried, along with all the seeds of our karma. After all, if we are only a surface consciousness that exists momentarily, where are all the memories of our past lives and all our karmic seeds stored? This is why it is called the "storehouse": In the Chittamatra system, all these things are stored there.

We have the six consciousnesses and the storehouse consciousness and then, between the two of them, the seventh consciousness, called the *klesha manovijnana,* meaning the "afflicted mind consciousness." In the Chittamatra system, this is considered to be the source of our sense of "I." It overlaps both the storehouse consciousness and our surface consciousness. So, whatever we do and say and think, "I"-ness is always there in the background.

The seventh consciousness is called the klesha manovijnana because, although it is a neutral consciousness, it is also an afflicted mental consciousness because the sense of self is the root of our delusion. Our sense of self is the root cause of afflictions like greed, anger, and envy—I want, I don't want. So it has that afflictive side. But it is also what is going to take us to awakening. It includes our aspirations, our desire to do good, our desire to practice. That is still based on ego, but at this point it is an ego that is working toward the good.

So this seventh consciousness, the source of our self identity, is actually considered neutral. It can go either way. Of course, this sense of "I" is given a bad rap in the Buddhist tradition, but nonetheless most of the Dharma deals with how to make use of our egocentric mind on the path until it can drop away. Therefore, it is important to cultivate a well-balanced, happy ego that is enthusiastic on the path, that wants to practice, and that wants to transform and transcend itself.

I remember when I was about eleven years old and we started learning physics in elementary school. I asked my physics teacher, "What is left when we reduce everything down and down—ultimately, what do we get?" She went on about protons and neutrons, but I thought, *No, because we must be able to further reduce that proton or neutron.* "Ultimately, what do you get at the end?" I asked, and she said that we can't reduce any more than that. So I lost interest in physics. I thought, *Scientists don't know*. But of course, on one level they do know. The fact is, however much we reduce something, we never can get to the thing in itself. Whether we call it light or energy or space, we can call it anything, but the thing in itself can never be found.

This is why His Holiness the Dalai Lama is so fascinated by science: because much of what scientists are revealing nowadays sounds like Madhyamaka, the higher philosophical tenet in Tibetan Buddhism. The scientists themselves are fascinated too. They say, "How can you do this? How can you have realized all this without having our huge laboratories and the billions of dollars spent on all these experiments? Just by sitting and looking at your mind, you have discovered that nothing has any self-existent reality?" And of course, the Madhyamaka scholars think, "How just by using machines could you have realized that nothing has any self-existent reality?" The fact that everything arises due to causes and conditions, that everything is interdependently originated, is what is called shunyata.

We make things seem solid and self-existent, but if we search we never can find them. It doesn't mean that things just disappear when we look for them and there's a big hole. It means that we can never find the thing in itself while our mind is projecting and reifying it. Author Michael Pollan puts it this way:

> [O]ur perceptions of the world offer us not a literal transcription of reality but rather a seamless illusion woven from both the data of our senses and the models in our memories. Normal waking consciousness feels perfectly transparent, and yet it is less a window on reality than the product of our imaginations—a kind of controlled hallucination.*

The point is, we live in a world that we are projecting, and we believe that how we perceive things is how they actually exist. But nothing is graspable. That includes our notion of ourselves: However much we seek this "I" that seems so embedded in us, we never can find it. If we look for it in our mind, the first

* Michael Pollan, *How to Change Your Mind: What the New Science of Psychedelics Teaches Us About Consciousness, Dying, Addiction, Depression, and Transcendence* (Penguin Press, 2018), 251–52.

thing that will happen is that the mind will seem to divide itself: There will be all the thoughts, the flow of the thoughts, and then the awareness that is watching the thoughts. So we might think, "Okay, drop the thoughts, and let's look at the awareness." But then the awareness itself cannot be grasped.

Most of meditation is about getting to understand our mind. If we are looking at the thoughts, who is looking? If we say, "I am looking," then who am "I"? It is like an onion. We unpeel layer after layer expecting a core, but there is no core. That was the Buddha's great insight. We are not who we think we are.

There is a story about Tsongkhapa, the founder of the Gelugpa order. He was teaching emptiness to an audience of about two thousand monks. At one point as he was talking, one monk clutched himself and kind of rolled over, and everybody started laughing. Tsongkhapa said, "No, don't laugh. He's the only one who's understood what I am saying." The monk had fallen into this state because suddenly his previous understanding of the self—of who he was at his core—was shattered. It can be quite alarming.

One time while I was living in my cave in Lahaul, a friend came to visit me. She was an artist, and she had been sitting outside sketching the mountains, and then she came staggering in. She was white and shaking. What had happened was that she was sketching the snow mountain, and then it moved. She realized it was not a mountain; it was a cloud. She was deeply shocked because something that had seemed so solid suddenly became so ephemeral, and she hadn't been able to tell the difference. She was completely shaken.

That is the point. If we truly understood what this is all about, we would all be shaking in shock. But it has to be understood, not by the intellect, but in the depths of our being. It's very radical. Our oh-so-solid world isn't solid at all. Nothing is solid, including ourselves. This brings us to the next aphorism in the second of Geshe Chekawa's seven points.

Regard Phenomena as If They Were Dreams

The next slogan says, *Regard phenomena as if they were dreams.* Consider that everything we experience is like a dream. All external phenomena, environments, and beings are nothing but apparitions of our deluded mind. Dreams seem very real, but on waking we can recognize they are delusory, only existing in our mind. Likewise, objects we encounter and our reactions to them are as transitory and unreal as dreams.

We think phenomena are far more concrete and tangible than they are. They are just the mental process of reification, of making something into a thing. It is just a process—everything is just an impermanent process—but we solidify it. We make it into something substantial and self-existing, just as we experience it to be. We slap a label on it and think our label is real. Then we either want the thing, don't want it, or feel indifferent toward it. But it will always arouse some emotion, often a negative emotion of either grasping or aversion. People do anything for things. Any phenomenon, such as a tree, a person, or the galaxy, depends on our mental designation for its existence; without this, it would not exist.

I read somewhere a report by a British neuroscientist, who said that something like 80 percent of what we apprehend through our senses is constructed by the brain. That is, what we actually receive through the senses is a small part. For example, if you see a dog, what your eyes are perceiving might be a vague, brown sort of object. Then, immediately, the mind will say, "Oh, that's a dog." After that, maybe it will specify a breed or a name. Immediately the mind, like a high-speed computer, creates an image that we then grasp at and believe in. This is what Geshe Chekawa is pointing to with this slogan: We think that what we apprehend through our senses exists precisely in the way that we see and experience it. But most of it is actually created by our minds.

We don't believe we are responsible for so much of what we perceive, but if we were animals with different kinds of senses, we would see everything quite differently. Dogs have a heightened perception of smells. They live in a world of scents, which is why a dog is always sniffing. Dogs know a whole world of scents that we have no idea about. Birds, fish, and all kinds of animals have their own special senses, and therefore they see and relate to the world in a very different way from humans. They are not less accurate than we are; they just have different senses.

If we had different senses or different sense levels than we do, if we had a different kind of brain that fits all that input together to make something we can relate to, we would see a different world. Things are not the way they seem to us, and most important, we are not the way we seem.

So again, it is like a dream. We believe our dreams while we are dreaming them. If it's a frightening dream, then our hearts are pounding. If it's a happy dream, we wake up happy. At that moment while we are dreaming, our body and mind believe the dream and react, just as you see dogs whimpering or growling in their sleep, their legs moving. We can see that they are dreaming that they are in a race or they are fighting with the neighboring dog or something else.

We believe it all too, until we wake up and realize it was mostly a dream created by our mind and senses. *Bodhi* means awakening; a buddha is someone who is awake. So, in some ways, rather than "enlightenment," the word *awakening* is a little more accurate, because we are trying to wake up from the dream of samsara.

When we say that it is like a dream, we are not saying that it all could go *poof* and disappear. When Geshe Chekawa says things are empty, he doesn't mean they don't exist. Shunyata doesn't mean emptiness in the sense of a vast void in which nothing really exists. What the text is saying is that things don't exist from their own side, as separate, static, unchanging, and self-existent entities. Things only exist in dependence on each other and in accordance with specific causes and conditions. For their existence, all phenomena that participate in natural laws depend on the causal conditions that gave rise to them: For example, the existence of sprouts depends on seeds, moisture, and warmth.

Even my eyeglasses exist because of a multitude of factors. Even the plastic of the frame exists because of many, many factors, including the people who made them, not to speak of all the materials, where the materials came from, the people who mined the materials, the people who processed the materials, who made the machines to process the materials, and so forth. It just goes on and on, and the interdependence includes more and more.

Everything we eat, every drop of water that we drink—how did it get here? It has so many causes—even just a mug of water, not to speak of the mug itself—both natural factors of its production and the people who were involved in it, plus all their antecedents. So this is the point, that everything depends on limitless factors. Every single thing arises from a limitless chain of causes and conditions. It's not that static, single thing that we think it is. Of course, this includes how we came into being, which is also dependent on a zillion causes. So that is also one meaning of the philosophical concept of emptiness, or nonself. What Geshe Chekawa is trying to say is that things are not self-existent, and they are not how they appear to be.

So much of our mental affliction comes from not understanding this. We wouldn't need this teaching if everything were fine, and we were all jolly, and everything was wonderful. But it isn't. People suffer so much. One of the reasons why we suffer is because we cling. Why do we cling? We cling because we believe in a self-existent, solid, enduring "I"; and solid, existent, enduring others; and solid, existent, enduring things that we either want or don't want. This causes so much suffering. It's not the things in themselves, it's the grasping. Things in themselves are innocent. The problem is our current state of mind seeing them as something that we cannot survive without. Due to that, we are in trouble.

So everything exists in interdependence with everything else, including ourselves. And everything comes together because of causes and conditions and is changing constantly. Every entity also has certain attributes, component parts, facets and qualities, and depends on these attributes for its existence. Again, we reify it, but actually anything that we look at has so many different facets and qualities, and it's the coming together of these qualities and attributes that we see. However, an entity or phenomenon is never equivalent to any one of its attributes, and it is not even the total sum of them; it is not *one* thing.

This is again complicated. The text says any entity has certain attributes, components, parts, facets, qualities. Take a flower. We think, "this is a flower." We can name it, and think it exists because it has a name. It has petals; it has pistils; it has a stem. It has color. It has a certain feel to its petals. It has many attributes that, when all together, collectively make what we call a flower. If we took a leaf off, we wouldn't say the leaf was a flower. If we took a petal off, we would say, "that's a petal." But neither is the flower a totality of these parts. If the pistil is missing, we don't say, "This is something entirely different from a flower." Then again, you cannot find a flower in the abstract, apart from its attributes. If you look for the flowerness of the flower, you cannot find it. It's just an agreed-upon custom, a convention if you will, to say that all this is going to be called a flower. This unfindability of the essence of the thing in itself is what is called shunyata, emptiness.

Another example: When we are looking at a mountain, it appears to exist from its own side. We just look out and say, "That is a mountain." But which part of it is the mountain? Every little grain of soil? The trees on it? The flowers? The snow? Where is the mountain-ness of the mountain? We imagine that there is an essential mountain. However, we usually don't see that the mountain exists depending on mental designations, depending on its attributes, and depending on its own causes and conditions. That's the point.

We designate, and that's fine. There's nothing wrong with designating and labeling. It's when we believe that something exists substantially from its own side just as it appears to us—that is the problem. Because an actual mountain, in itself, is unfindable except as a conglomeration of all its various attributes, including the label or name *mountain*. Therefore, we should avoid the two extremes, of thinking everything exists just as we perceive it and of thinking nothing exists, which is nihilism. The Buddha said, "I too use conceptual language, but I am not fooled by it."

And that is the difference: We are totally fooled by it. So we should pray again and again to be able to see things as they really are.

Examine the Unborn Nature of Awareness

The next slogan is, *Examine the unborn nature of awareness.* We are still discussing ultimate bodhichitta. The last slogan was mainly dealing with external phenomena, the fact that we cannot find a thing in itself, that everything is due to causes and conditions and has no inherent self-existence that we can point to and definitively say, this is it. However much we look for the thing, it just keeps turning into something else. Now we are taking that awareness that analyzes external reality and external beings and turning it back on ourselves. We are examining the nature of unborn awareness.

We have a mind that analyzes all these external phenomena, but when examined, the mind that just did the analysis does not exist. Even in the present, the mind cannot be found. We cannot grasp our awareness and say, "This is awareness," because it has already gone, meaning it is empty of identifiable characteristics. We cannot say: "This is mind. I've got it, now, I've caught it." The mind is ungraspable. Past mind, gone. Future mind, not come. Present mind—by the time we say present mind, it's already gone.

The perceiving mind, the mind that is conscious, that is aware, is said to abide as "primordially unborn." In this tradition, all thoughts, feelings, emotions, and sensations are categorized simply as "thought." Anger, greed, happiness, and sorrow are all just thoughts. All are part of the conceptual mind, the surface of the mind. If we think of the mind as an ocean, then these are the surface waves. The surface waves of emotions rise up, go down, up, down. It is just at the surface of the mind. They are all just thoughts; none of them are the mind itself. Mind has no color or form. It is not a thing. We cannot catch the mind. So then, rest in that experience of openness and non-discursiveness without an attempt to label or define it. That is the empty nature of the mind.

So what is mind really? The first thing we notice about our mind is our thoughts. We are always incessantly thinking. Often people are not even conscious of how noisy and busy their mind is until they sit down to meditate. Often the first thing that people who try to meditate will report is that through meditation their minds have gotten worse: They are having more thoughts than ever; their minds are much noisier than they used to be. But of course, it is not that their mind is becoming noisier or that they are thinking more. They are simply becoming more conscious of that inner noise.

It is as if we have a radio or television playing constantly inside our mind the whole time we are sitting. It is rather like how some people keep their television on all the time just for the sound in the background. That's our mind. A mental television is always on inside our minds, and we can't seem to turn it down. Normally, we are not so conscious of the noise because we are just going along with it. As soon as we try to stand back from this inner TV program, then we are conscious that there is really a big problem here. Where's the control button?

Not only are we unable to turn down the volume, once we start looking at the programs, we see they are an endless series of soap operas, with all these reruns. We are not conscious of that normally. But of course, it is the first problem that comes up as soon as we try to quiet the mind or become more conscious of what is going on inside. We realize we are totally the slave of our thoughts. We are not the masters of our own mind, and yet we have to take our mind with us everywhere we go.

Our perceptions of external reality are thoughts, and our internal memories, ideas, beliefs, feelings, and sense of identification are also thoughts. People kill and die for their beliefs, but a belief is just a thought. Our whole life is driven by our thinking—all our decisions, all our ideas, all our beliefs are part of our mind stream. Our mind is where we live, and we take it with us everywhere we go. We can never be separated from our mind. Even in our dreams, we are in our mind. And yet the mind is the thing that is most strange to us. So we must become familiar with our own mind.

This is what meditation is all about. Meditation is about learning who we really are. We start with the obvious—that we have thoughts. Feelings come up, we look at them, and we recognize that they are not the solid entities they appear to be. They are like bubbles. A bubble is very bright and shiny, but then, *pop*, it is completely empty. Our thoughts are like that. They are like bubbles on a stream. They are just bubbles. We don't have to believe in them.

Understanding this, we begin to create the ability not to be swamped by the mind, not to be swept along by our conceptual thoughts and feelings. It's not that we stop thinking. In Tibetan Buddhism especially, we are very kind about the thoughts. Thoughts are not the problem. Thoughts are not an enemy. It is our identification with the thoughts that is the problem. We create the sense of "I" through our thinking. This is the problem.

In meditation, after we have got the mind calmed down and more focused, after we have developed better attention skills, we are able to rest the awareness where we want it to rest. It is not running all over the place. Then we can start to look at the mind. For example, we focus our attention on the breath, then we turn it back onto the mind itself. It is like we sit back and just watch the show.

The traditional example is of someone sitting on a riverbank watching the water go by. In this analogy, the stream of thoughts is like the river—constantly flowing—and that is what we observe. The person doesn't jump in the river and get swept along. With our thoughts, however, we are usually engrossed in them. So as soon as we recognize that we are being swept along by the river again, we climb back out to the bank. We make the thought stream the object of the meditation. And then if one does that, one begins to really see it's like a movie being projected.

If you think of a movie being projected, you have the screen and you have the movie. In this movie, we are usually playing the starring role. In fact, we are both the audience and the movie. But the thing is, when we watch a good film our emotions respond as if it were real: If it is frightening, our heart races, for example. But the minute we say to ourselves, "This is just a movie," then we can relax and enjoy it. We are not going to go into true grief at the end when the hero dies; we know it is just an act. In the past, movies were projected by shining light onto reels of film—little transparent frames that are moving very fast. The light that is shining through those frames projects what appears to be the reality on the screen. That is also a fairly good analogy of what is happening with our minds.

Our unborn awareness is also sometimes called the clear light nature of the mind. That luminosity shines through all these transparent mental frames of our conscious mind and projects outward our whole reality. If we see life and everything out here as a nice 3D movie, then we are fine. We can enjoy the show. It is only when we really believe in appearances that we are in trouble. So, in order to really understand this movie is just the play of appearances, we need to recognize the projector that is the clear light nature of the mind.

The Buddha himself said that if there were not the unconditioned, there would be no conditioned, nor could there be escape from the conditioned. The conditioned here means our ordinary, conceptual mind. Behind that conceptual mind is the unconditioned mind, which is the pure, primordial, unborn awareness that we all share.

Another metaphor is the nature of the sky. There is a huge, vast, infinite sky, but we get caught up in the clouds. During the monsoon season in India, for example, all we see are thick clouds, and we forget that they reside in a much bigger sky. Those clouds could not exist if it were not for the clear, empty sky. The clouds arise in the sky, and they go back into the sky; in fact, they are the sky. Likewise, everything that we think is permeated by pure awareness. We don't recognize it, because we are caught in the clouds. Because of the dense flow of thoughts, we are not conscious of being conscious.

What we need to do is step back: First we become aware of the ordinary thinking mind. Then we look into the awareness that illuminates this thinking mind. What is watching the thoughts? We rest in that.

At first it is a duality: the watcher and the watched. But, if we continue to look at the watcher, it eventually, of itself, opens up into the expanse of pure nondual awareness, and this transcends the duality of observer and observed. The first step is to cultivate that awareness in the mind, so to speak, where we are observing the thoughts without being the thoughts. Then we can open up the level of awareness that is not creating the divide between self and other. Anybody can do this, because that is the way the mind functions: The mind is nondual by its nature. It really is like waking up from the dream of habitual duality.

The problem is that we wake up like this for an instant and then we fall asleep again. However, there is a point at which one awakens and remains awake. There have been great masters throughout the ages in all spiritual traditions who have woken up once and for all. The point to remember is that nondual primordial awareness is who we truly are. We are awakened beings. We already have all the qualities of an enlightened being. It is just that, at the present moment, we are snoozing. It might be a very long sleep, but our original nature is still to be awake. We are not trying to acquire something from out there; we are trying to discover something within.

We already have this ultimate bodhichitta—which is the nature of our unborn awareness—but it is covered over. The traditional example is of a beggar living in a hut while, beneath his floor, there is a huge treasure—maybe a flawless diamond. He doesn't know it is there, so the beggar goes out every day to beg for coins. He thinks he is poor, but all the time he is a multimillionaire. He is just not looking for wealth in the right place. All of us already have all the fullness of our true nature. This is why samsara is a tragedy. We recognize our genuine potential, which is so fantastic, but what are we doing with it?

This is also why great wisdom comes together with compassion: The more we begin to wake up, the more we see how everyone is sleeping, and we feel so sad. Sometimes when we look into the eyes of someone, we see so much suffering, but we know it is unnecessary because we are all buddhas. If only we could wake up. We have such great potential for awakening, but very few will put in the effort to awaken. We waste our lives in suffering because of that. So compassion is not just for the poor, the sick, and sad little puppies. We also have compassion for our condition as human beings. Naturally great compassion arises when we see what a state we have all put ourselves in, which isn't even necessary.

This is our problem, so we have to wake up. This is all we have to do. We have to stop identifying with the wrong things and start investigating and opening ourselves up to what is genuine within ourselves instead of what is counterfeit. The good news is that, throughout the millennia, there are people who have done this. Of course, most of them we never hear about, but we are very fortunate that some of them, like Geshe Chekawa, have left us roadmaps to follow.

The practice of reconnecting with our true nature is like finding a water source. We dig down and down, and at first the ground seems very dry, but eventually the soil begins to get a little moist. We feel encouraged, so we keep digging. Then, finally, we connect with a vast underground lake, and the water just comes gushing up.

Buddhism sometimes looks negative, always going on about

the "I" and how bad it is. It is important to remember: This is only because the Dharma is trying to tell us not to rely on our false identification. We are actually so much greater than we think. This is the ultimate bodhichitta. Ultimate bodhichitta is our essential buddhahood. This is who we truly are.

The rest of *The Seven-Point Mind-Training* deals mostly with relative bodhichitta and how to deal with our egos and habitual behaviors in a useful way—that is, how to take everything onto the path. But we must not forget the ultimate bodhichitta. This is why the author starts with this: how things really are. Until we realize that, he is saying, these are the other things we can practice. But the essential point is that we already have everything that we are seeking. We already are who we want to be. We just can't see it yet.

The last important thing to remember about the nature of unborn awareness is that, when we do experience that awareness, we should just rest in it. We shouldn't try to define it or grasp it. We shouldn't try to think about it or analyze it. We should just recognize it and relax.

Even the Remedy Itself Is Free Right Where It Is

The next slogan is, *Even the remedy itself is free right where it is*. If we cling to emptiness, it becomes just another attachment that causes suffering. This slogan is telling us that to remedy this, we must understand that even emptiness is empty. We must not reify the idea of shunyata or make it into another "thing" to cling to. We shouldn't grasp with the mind at anything—even emptiness is empty of inherent nature. Therefore, the remedy naturally liberates itself, freed in its own place.

The commentary explains that any thought or remedy, including the thought of emptiness, is itself empty by nature, or without substantial existence. Therefore, we must not cling to experiences and realizations. For example, when we have some experience—maybe of emptiness, bliss, or the nature of the mind—we often think, "Ah, this is the real thing!" and we try to hold on to it. We want that experience again and again. But in doing this, the ego takes over. The ego tries to make the experience into something it can grasp. However, even our experiences and realizations must self-liberate. We can't cling to them. If we do, we have lost them again. We are back to conceptual thinking.

It is important not to make the idea of emptiness or pure awareness into another object to grasp onto. We must recognize that emptiness itself is empty. Otherwise, we remain caught in an endless circle of thinking.

Resting in the Universal Ground Is the Essential Nature of the Path

The text then states, *Resting in the universal ground is the essential nature of the path.* The Chittamatra tradition explains that the eighth consciousness, the *alaya vijnana,* is the substratum consciousness, the repository of all memories and of the seeds, or impulses, of karma. This is where everything is stored—the storehouse consciousness.

In the Chittamatra tradition, the seven consciousnesses and the eighth—the alaya vijnana—are usually understood as the repository of all impressions. The alaya vijnana is often defined on two levels. On the relative level, it is like the bottom of the ocean, where everything sinks. But in this context, alaya vijnana is at the universal level, synonymous with the dharmakaya. *Dharmakaya* literally means "Dharma body," referring to the ultimate, formless nature of a buddha, the absolute truth or reality beyond all dualistic appearances. In Mahayana and Vajrayana Buddhism, the dharmakaya is one of the three bodies of a buddha. It is sometimes described as pure being or buddha nature, the timeless, all-encompassing reality that all beings ultimately share.

Alaya is the immediate present, which is the only moment we have. As soon as we grasp it, it is gone. The past is finished, and the future hasn't arrived. So this continuous immediate present combined with pure *vijnana,* awareness, is synonymous with the clear light nature of the mind. This alaya vijnana—the clear light nature or buddha nature or dharmakaya mind—is beyond all mental elaborations and conceptual proliferations. It is a clarity beyond clinging and conceptualization.

Thus, the instruction is to rest in the empty nature of the mind—the awareness of awareness. Our problem is that we are not conscious of being conscious. We are not aware of being aware. Of course, if we totally lacked awareness we wouldn't be able to think, but we are so busy thinking that we cannot recognize our actual, pure awareness. It is like looking up at the sky but seeing only clouds. The blue sky must be there—otherwise, there could be no clouds—but we don't see it. We have to part the clouds to see the sky.

When we practice the following meditation, the sessions should be short and intense, with many sub-sessions. The untrained mind cannot sustain prolonged periods of resting in pure awareness without becoming tired and dispersed. Short, focused sessions allow the mind to experience its natural state without getting lost in conceptual proliferation. If we hold on too long, the mind starts proliferating again, and we lose the clarity.

Resting and relaxing into awareness means not thinking anything or doing anything. The meditation has no object. Typically, when we meditate, we focus on something: our breath, an object, a visualization, a mantra, or even the mind itself. In this practice, awareness rests within itself. There is no object. The awareness does not focus on anything external. It just relaxes into its own nature. Again, this state is difficult to sustain for long periods unless one is highly skilled and advanced. So it is better to keep sessions short and have many of them rather than forcing the mind for too long.

This approach is similar to Soto Zen meditation, where the focus is on simply being—relaxing into the state of presence without doing anything; whatever arises is allowed to come and go without any clinging, hoping, or fearing. This practice is about returning to the essential level of pure awareness and relaxing into it. The meditation progresses from observing thoughts to examining the nature of unborn awareness to, finally, resting in this nondual awareness. The essential path is to rest in pure awareness.

Between Sessions, Be an Illusory Person

The next slogan states, *Between sessions, be an illusory person.* In other words, in the intervals between your meditation sessions, view oneself, other people, and all phenomena as illusory or dreamlike, like a movie or a hologram. Remaining mindful in this way ensures that our practice is untainted by grasping at real entities.

It is important, however, not to fall into indifference in daily life. Recognizing the illusory nature of reality does not mean dismissing others' suffering or becoming devoid of empathy. In fact, great beings have greater compassion and a naturally flowing kindness. Recognizing the illusory nature of life should not result in emotional detachment or a sense of separation as if we were looking at life through a pane of glass. Indeed, this awareness connects us with all living beings. At the same time, it should free us from taking things so desperately seriously, especially when bad things happen to us.

Ultimately, we are like conjurers who create wonderful illusions but still know they are tricks. By understanding this, we avoid being endlessly tossed about on the waves of life. Mindfulness becomes the boat that helps us navigate life skillfully. Positive emotions like compassion, loving-kindness, and empathy should be cultivated, while negative emotions like anger, despair, grief, and rage are seen as projections we need not respond to. These negative emotions don't help us, and recognizing them as illusions gives us freedom.

This concludes the first part of *The Seven-Point Mind-Training* that focused on ultimate bodhichitta, or how to experience reality from the perspective of emptiness and non-ego—that is, how a highly realized being views themself and outer phenomena. The rest of the text discusses training in conventional bodhichitta, so now we will move on to what the rest of us—those of us still caught up in our egos—can do and how we can use bodhichitta on the path.

Alternately Practice Giving and Taking; Mount Them Both upon Your Breath

Of course, when most people think of lojong they automatically associate it with the practice of *tonglen*. In Tibetan, *tong* means to send, and *len* means to receive. So tonglen is the practice of sending and accepting, giving and taking. And here the text says, *Alternately practice giving and taking*. Then the next slogan is, *Mount them both upon your breath*. (Sometimes the order is reversed.) I'll cover both of these together.

The practice of tonglen entails visualizing oneself taking on the sickness and suffering of others and replacing it with one's own well-being, good fortune, and all positive qualities. Essentially, it is the practice of relative bodhichitta—the idea that, if we could, we would take on all the sufferings of the world and replace them with happiness.

Tonglen is a practical means of cultivating loving-kindness and compassion. Loving-kindness is the wish, *May all beings be happy*, and compassion is the wish, *May they be free from suffering*. Tonglen combines these two aspirations into a single practice by taking in the suffering of others and sending out all that is good and wholesome.

This practice was originally considered too difficult and too counterintuitive to human nature to be widely taught. At first, it was shared only with a few close disciples of the lama teaching it, because it was seen as too challenging for most people, since our egoic nature tends to prioritize our own happiness and regard others' suffering as "their problem." However, Geshe Chekawa and Langri Tangpa later opened it up so that more people could learn it. Despite these early concerns that reflect a low estimation of human potential, tonglen has become one of the most popular Tibetan Buddhist practices and is now embraced across all lineages.

Many high lamas have noted that tonglen is an especially helpful practice during illness or the dying process. When asked what practices they are doing generally, lamas often reply, "tonglen." Tonglen has also become popular among certain Catholic monks and nuns, many of whom have requested teachings on it and find it profoundly helpful. This practice resonates naturally with people on a spiritual path, as it taps into a deep sense of empathy and interconnection.

The basic idea of this practice is to focus on someone who is suffering. If the person is physically present—perhaps during a hospital visit—it can make the practice feel more immediate. It is often easiest to begin with someone for whom we feel a heartfelt connection, such as a loved one. For example, we might think of someone who is ill, grieving, or experiencing mental distress.

The text instructs us to "mount them [i.e., giving and taking] upon your breath," which ties the slogans together. On the in-breath, we visualize drawing in all the suffering, misery, and sickness of someone in particular and even the karmic causes and conditions behind that suffering. You can imagine this suffering as dark light or smoke—whatever resonates with you—and breathe it in so it drops to the center of the chest. Here, we can visualize there is a small black pearl representing the self-cherishing mind that prioritizes itself above all else and thinks, "I'm sorry you're suffering, but I'm glad it's not me." This self-cherishing mind resists taking on the suffering of others. Yet, by consciously breathing in their suffering, we strike directly at this hard knot of egoic self-concern. When the dark smoke of suffering reaches the black pearl on the in-breath, that hard knot immediately transforms.

The black pearl dissolves to reveal the true nature of the mind, which can be visualized as a diamond. This diamond represents buddha nature—our pure awareness. Buddha nature is inherently pure and untainted. No matter how much darkness or negativity we encounter, it cannot pollute the mind's true nature, just as the sky remains untouched by passing clouds. This realization gives us confidence: No matter how much suffering we breathe in, it cannot harm our fundamental purity.

On the out-breath, the transformed diamond radiates outward as white or golden light. This light represents all goodness, well-being, and positive qualities. It saturates the being of the person you are visualizing, filling every cell and layers of their consciousness with healing and happiness. This light symbolizes the infinite goodness within us. Like the sky, our true nature is boundless and unlimited—an inexhaustible resource. Giving away your goodness does not deplete it; there is always more.

This is the basic tonglen practice, and it can be extraordinarily powerful. It might feel artificial at first, and we may feel some internal resistance, questioning whether we are truly managing to take on others' suffering. This resistance only reveals the workings of the self-cherishing mind, which makes the practice deeply insightful. To begin, however, it is often helpful to focus on someone for whom we already feel a willingness to sacrifice ourselves, such as a child, a parent, or someone to whom we feel immense gratitude.

We can also apply tonglen to our own suffering. For instance, if we are ill, we can imagine taking on the suffering of all the others in the world who share our condition. We might think: "May their suffering come to me. I will bear it for them. May they be free from this pain." This transforms our illness into an opportunity for compassion and connection, shifting the focus from self-pity to altruism. Similarly, if we are grieving, we can connect with the pain of others who have experienced loss and take their grief upon ourselves, wishing them relief.

Through tonglen we uncover layers of interconnection, compassion, and empathy. We begin to realize that our suffering is not unique but shared. This recognition deepens our sense of connection to others. The practice also shifts our perspective, helping us to move beyond self-centered concerns and even use obstacles as opportunities for growth and for developing compassion.

Ultimately, tonglen embodies the essence of the lojong approach: transforming obstacles into profound opportunities for practice. What initially seems difficult or counterintuitive becomes a powerful method for awakening bodhichitta, developing altruism, and connecting deeply with the interdependent nature of all beings.

Three Objects, Three Poisons, and Three Roots of Virtue

The next slogan is, *Three objects, three poisons, and three roots of virtue*. This is straightforward. The three objects are sensory experiences—all sights, sounds, smells, tastes, and touches—that we find attractive, unattractive, or neutral. Every object we encounter falls into one of these categories: We either like it, we don't like it, or we feel indifferent. There is no other option.

Objects here refer to sense objects—what is perceived by the eyes, ears, nose, tongue, and the rest of the body. These objects—attractive, unattractive, and neutral—give rise to the three poisons: desire, aversion, and delusion. When we find an object attractive, the mind reaches out and wants to grasp it, which leads to greed and attachment. When the object is unpleasant to us, it triggers aversion, irritation, or the urge to push it away. If the object is neutral, we can be unmindful and indifferent to it, which is a deluded state of mind.

If we engage with the three objects without mindfulness, they become gateways to these poisonous states of mind. Therefore, we must guard the gates of the senses. This doesn't mean we cannot enjoy things, but it reminds us to enjoy them without grasping or becoming greedy. Similarly, we don't have to love everything, but when we encounter something unpleasant, we can recognize it as such without letting it lead to anger, aversion, or emotional disturbance. We can simply observe, "This is pleasant," or "This is unpleasant," without reacting emotionally. Regarding ignorance, we can acknowledge our own interpretations of things, people, and situations, and become aware that they lack intrinsic qualities and, at the same time, are deeply interconnected with everything else.

Further, the three roots of virtue will counter the three poisons. These are loving-kindness, compassion, and equanimity. Loving-kindness is the wish that all beings be happy; this counteracts selfish desire. Compassion is the wish that all beings be free from suffering; this counteracts aversion. And equanimity allows us to meet all experiences with balance and impartiality; this avoids delusion.

The practice encourages this aspiration: *May the obscurations of all beings, arising from the three poisons, come upon me as a load to bear. May all the negative thoughts caused by attachment, aggres-*

sion, and delusion come to me. I will bear them. May all beings live virtuously, perform positive deeds, and be free from the three poisons.

This extends the tonglen practice from taking on others' physical sicknesses and grief to their mental poisons as well. We take on the mental afflictions of others, recognizing their empty nature. Although this might sound burdensome, realizing the vacuity of these poisons and grounding ourselves in the roots of virtue makes the load light. We take the poisons upon ourselves and transform them, wishing all beings freedom and a peaceful mind. Wouldn't that be wonderful? *May all beings have happy, peaceful minds.*

In Everything You Do, Practice with Words

The text continues, *In everything you do, practice with words.* This means using maxims or slogans in daily life to transform ordinary actions into the path. For example: *May the sufferings of all beings ripen upon me. Through my virtues, may they achieve happiness.* Think such thoughts throughout the day during all activities.

We can incorporate this practice into everyday life. When opening a door, think: *May I open the door to liberation for all beings,* or *May the door of liberation be open for all beings.* When sitting down, think: *May all beings be seated on the seat of enlightenment.* When eating, think: *May all beings be nourished by virtuous deeds.* By creating personal slogans, we can transform ordinary actions into mindfulness practices and turn them into acts of virtue.

This practice isn't just about refraining from negative actions or performing positive deeds. It turns even neutral, mundane actions into steps on the path to enlightenment. Bringing mindfulness into ordinary moments connects us with the Dharma throughout the day. Otherwise, we risk becoming mindless, thinking only formal practice or Dharma teachings count as "real practice," while the rest of the day feels like tedious worldly activity. But this mindset can change. With effort, even the most mundane tasks can sparkle with meaning.

For example, when washing or bathing, imagine washing away all your negative karmic imprints. We might say the Vajrasattva mantra while visualizing ourselves becoming free from negative patterns. This approach integrates the Dharma into daily life. Thinking up meaningful slogans and reminders for different activities keeps us connected to our purpose, transforming the ordinary into the extraordinary.

Begin the Training Sequence with Yourself

The next slogan says, *Begin the training sequence with yourself.* The practice also suggests beginning with oneself. This is a very crucial point. All lojong texts mention, at some point, that the practice of tonglen must start with ourselves. The Buddha taught that, in order to practice meditation, we need a well-balanced sense of self. A balanced self is one that is not completely dominated by the three poisons (desire, anger, and ignorance) and that is good-hearted, kind, and calm. A balanced sense of self is not neurotic or traumatized. Feelings of self-loathing or low self-esteem are not balanced either. Tonglen, practiced for ourselves, heals all these issues. Once that healing is achieved, then we can begin practicing meditation and building a foundation of tranquility and one-pointedness.

Also, when taking on the sufferings of others feels overwhelming, you can start by practicing tonglen for yourself. Imagine your teacher or the Buddha at your heart center radiating virtue, well-being, wisdom, and compassion. Give all your negativity to them. Let them absorb it and transform it, radiating light back to us. This visualization connects us with our buddha nature, represented by the teacher, *yidam* (meditational deity), or Buddha at our heart.

If one is feeling particularly depressed or overwhelmed, this practice can be very helpful. We can visualize our suffering being taken in and transformed by the Buddha or our teacher, who represents our true nature. If we struggle with unresolved childhood trauma or painful memories, we might visualize our younger self as a small child and practice tonglen for them. This can help heal and integrate past pain by replacing it with well-being and compassion.

The beauty of tonglen is its flexibility. We can use it in countless ways. The important thing is to find what works for you. The essence of the practice is to take in suffering and dissolve it, replacing it with well-being. If starting with yourself feels easier, do that. Build confidence and visualization skills and, when ready, extend the practice to others.

Ultimately, lojong practice aims to move us beyond self-preoccupation and self-importance. It takes courage to wish deeply for the happiness of others and to dedicate oneself to relieving their pain. The lojong teachings remind us that the happiness of billions of beings far outweighs the concerns of one individual. Recognizing this, we can let go of the constant "me, me, me" and open our hearts to others with genuine compassion.

3

THE THIRD POINT

Transforming Adversity into an Aid to Spiritual Awakening

Point three is about taking adverse conditions onto the path of enlightenment. This is the very essence of the lojong attitude to life. As Apo Rinpoche, a very high lama in the Drukpa Kagyu tradition, said: "If you say obstacle, it is an obstacle. If you say opportunity, it becomes an opportunity."

When the Whole World Is Enslaved by Vices, Transform Adversities into the Path of Spiritual Awakening

The first slogan under this point reads, *When the whole world is enslaved by vices, transform adversities into the path of spiritual awakening*. The various commentaries explain that all adverse situations caused by other beings or natural elements—nature itself—are the result of past karma. Those unfamiliar with the Dharma would view these situations as obstacles or misfortunes.

Dharma practitioners, however, transform them into practice by reflecting: *Since beginningless time, I have failed to distinguish what is to be relinquished and what is to be adopted. Whatever spiritual practices I have adopted have been expressions of self-grasping, leaving me with no enduring experience of liberation. From today, I will view my self-cherishing mind as the enemy and all sentient beings as my friends.*

This teaching of transforming adverse conditions into the path of enlightenment is central to lojong. When we encounter difficulties caused by other people or circumstances, instead of thinking, "Oh, this is my bad karma," and feeling sorry for ourselves—or, more likely, blaming others—we transform these challenges into practice.

We often think, "I could really practice, if only . . ." There is always an "if only." This teaching shows us that the real obstacle is our self-cherishing mind. Without self-cherishing, there would be no obstacle. So we turn difficulties and adversities into the path of enlightenment. But how? Geshe Chekawa's text goes on to provide instructions, but the essence of them is this: Everything that happens—whether from our own defilements, others' actions, or external events like natural disasters—is an opportunity for practice. These challenges are not detours; they *are* the path. It's not a smooth, easy road.

People often think that when things go wrong, they are off the path. But what is the path? The path is our ability to deal with whatever arises and turn it into practice. This is a vital point, because it frees us from hope and fear. We hope things will go as we want and fear they won't, which leads to anxiety. But perhaps it's better when things don't go as planned. Challenges—illnesses, personal conflicts, and difficulties—are where we grow from.

We imagine a good life is one full of pleasure, comfort, and success. If our life is filled with difficulties, disappointments, or ill health, we think we have failed. But this view is based on ego. If life were only about being comfortable, well-fed, and adored, we might as well pray to come back as a pet poodle—pampered and worry-free. Instead, we must ask ourselves, "What is this life for?" Someone once said life is the gymnasium of the soul. Though Buddhism doesn't speak of a soul, the metaphor applies. Life is where we learn. If lessons are too easy, we learn little. Growth comes from challenges that stretch us beyond what we think is possible.

I once went to a lama with complaints about obstacles. He told me, "You say it's an obstacle. I say it's an opportunity." This is the essence of the teaching. Obstacles are obstacles because we label them so. If instead we say, "This is my chance to strengthen my practice," then we learn. Looking back, most people realize that times of difficulty were when they learned the most. This doesn't mean we wish suffering on anyone. But when challenges arise, they reveal whether we are true practitioners. In good times, we are all love and light. But when things fall apart, our practice is tested.

It is like going to a gym. Lifting light weights won't build strength. To grow strong, we must lift heavy weights. The same is true for the mind and spirit. Without challenges, we become complacent, mistaking intellectual study or retreat experiences for true practice. Then, when life falls apart, we are unprepared. Many people say, "I had such deep insights during retreat, and I was so blissful . . . until I went back to my family." This is the test: Real practice happens in ordinary life—within our families, relationships, and workplaces. It's not just about maintaining peace when things are easy. It is about meeting difficulties skillfully and with strength.

The essence of lojong is in this verse: *When the whole world is enslaved by vices, transform adversities into the path of awakening.* This is our opportunity. Instead of resenting difficulties, we can feel almost grateful for the chance to apply what we've learned. When problems arise, this is our test. Will we feel sorry for ourselves or rise to the challenge? We must ask, "What can I learn?"

As the saying goes, *When the going gets tough, the tough get going.* This modern slogan echoes lojong's essence. Self-pity has no place here. We created the conditions we now face—if not recently, then in the past. What happens to us is the result of our actions, even if we don't remember. Blaming others or feeling victimized doesn't help. Instead, we take responsibility and see all our challenges as teachings.

How we respond actually determines whether a difficulty is an obstacle or an opportunity. The choice is ours: Will we sink into despair, or transform our experience into practice?

Blame Everything on One Culprit

The next slogan is, *Blame everything on one culprit.* All suffering, all sickness, the loss of wealth, lawsuits, and so on are all the result of clinging to "I." This is where we should place the blame for all our mishaps. All suffering arises through our clinging to the ego. We should not blame anything on others.

We cling to the "I" when in fact there is nothing to cling to. This is our basic delusion. If we had no ego clinging, there would be no problem. And so everything that happens, instead of saying, "It's your fault," we must recognize we are seeing it as a problem only because of our ego clinging.

The problem isn't out *there*, the problem is in *here*—which is good news, isn't it? Because we cannot change anybody else, but with a bit of work, we could change ourselves. We could stop endlessly thinking, "It's his fault, it's her fault, it's the fault of the government, it's the fault of this, it's the fault of that." We could stop thinking it's always somebody else out there and it is never us.

It is like people giving an account of a quarrel. "Well, I just said this and this. But then, *he* said that and that! I was so reasonable. Why did he get so upset?" And then we hear his side, and it comes out the same way: "I was being so understanding and reasonable, but she said *that*!" It is always the same: The blame is out there. It is always on the other person. But it is not about the other person. Whatever they do, that is their problem. Our problem is that we resent it. We put the blame on them. The moment we stop trying to change the external conditions and instead make an attempt to change our own mind, that in itself can trigger a major change in our lives.

On the other hand, it might seem so much more spiritual to blame everything difficult that happens on ourselves. But we should be careful here. Nowadays, many people look very confident outwardly, but inwardly they feel fragile. And so it is easy for them to take all this talk about the obstacle of self-cherishing and about putting all the blame on oneself as another excuse for beating themselves over the head, bringing their low self-esteem even lower. So we have to be very careful of what we mean here.

Shantideva said that there is a big distinction between arrogance or pride, which is a mental defilement, and self-confidence, which is essential for the path. So, when our teachers are beating us up about our ego clinging and our self-cherishing mind, they are not trying to undercut our self-confidence or our belief in our ability to practice and gain insight and enlightenment.

It is important that we don't use these teachings as a way to make ourselves feel useless or inferior. This is important. The idea that "I"-ness is the culprit is not meant to make us feel worse, so that any time we have any joy, we think, "Oh, I mustn't be happy, because that's my self-cherishing mind." It doesn't mean that. Nobody is jollier than the great masters. They are always laughing. What it means is that we are trying to step out of our obsession with *me,* because from a Buddhist point of view, pride doesn't just mean thinking, "I'm better than someone else." It also means thinking, "I'm just as good as someone else," or "I'm inferior to someone else." It is all pride. Why? Because it's still all about "I." If we think we are the lowest worm in the world or we imagine we are godlike, it is still all about "I."

Beating the ego with low self-regard doesn't kill the ego. We just get a cringing, sad little ego. There is nothing more difficult to deal with than a sad, cringing ego. The only way to dissolve the ego is by recognizing, by actually experiencing deeply, the ego's inherently empty nature and by opening up into a state of consciousness beyond the ego.

Again, these teachings are not intended to make us feel bad about ourselves. They are intended to make us stop thinking so much about ourselves and more about other beings. We can think how wonderful it is that other beings are sometimes really horrible to us, and in this way they enable us to learn patience and compassion. Without others being horrible, how could we learn? So we are grateful to all beings.

The important thing is just to step out of the way, to be more alive to others and less obsessed with our own self. This is what these teachings are about. Therefore, when it says, *Blame everything on one culprit,* this means our self-absorption, this obsession that we have with "me" the whole time. My ideas, my thoughts, my worries, my troubles, my horrible childhood, my hopes, my fears—endlessly caught up in ourselves.

This is why psychoanalysis is so popular. We pay someone to sit there while we talk and talk about ourselves. I have hardly met a single American who has not had a therapist. Like having a dentist, everybody has their therapist. Please understand, the ego is perfectly happy to be miserable. This is important. We think that the ego only wants to be happy, but really the ego only wants to exist. If we are miserable, we are only continually thinking, "me, me, me," and that's what the ego likes. We are not even interested in other people and their suffering; we are only interested in our own.

People who are psychologically disturbed can only talk about themselves; they couldn't care less about anybody else. One of the treatments for psychological problems is getting the patient to do work for others who are in even worse trouble, just to break out of this prison of "me." A healthily balanced mind takes care of itself, of course, but at the same time it is very interested in other people. Learning about other people can be much more interesting than being constantly absorbed in oneself.

So we should look at our thoughts. What are we really thinking about most of the time? Is it the welfare of others, or is it all about "me"? We think if we could only satisfy ourselves sufficiently, we would be happy. But we never can. It is like this huge black hole; it can never be filled. It can never be satisfied, no matter what we do, and this is what causes our suffering. The only thing to do is relax it, to just let go.

When we are balanced human beings, we definitely take care of ourselves. We need to be fed, we need to be clothed, we need to be housed. We are animals, so we need these basic things to sustain our bodies. But what are we going to do with the rest of our lives? This is the question.

We might put a lot of effort into our spiritual life, but then—after we recite so many mantras, offer so many prostrations, undertake so many retreats, study so many Dharma books, go and see so many lamas, get so many empowerments—at the end of twenty or thirty years, we might look back and realize we are basically still the same, if not worse. So then we say, "What went wrong?" So we really have to think about this. Does the Dharma actually encourage more self-absorption? In that case it is increasing the sickness instead of being a cure. If we use up our spiritual life just maintaining an obsession with ourselves, then it is just not going to work.

The Dalai Lama often says that the aim of Dharma is really to cultivate the good heart. We are aspiring to realize the nature of the mind and cultivate pure perception, but nonetheless, do we have a good heart? Each one of us has to ask ourselves, are we actually even nicer people? Forget how many empowerments we have received, how many lamas we have met. Has it actually helped?

Many years ago, I was in Lahaul when the Dalai Lama came for the first time. He gave talks and empowerments for about three days there. At the end of it all, I spoke with a Lahauli woman and asked, "Did you understand what the Dalai Lama was talking about?" She replied, "Well, I didn't really catch much, but I did understand: 'If you have a good heart, well done!'" So that is the point. That much we could all get from practicing the Dharma. Whether or not we gain great experiences, whether we get profound realizations, whether we go leaping from *bhumi* to *bhumi*, up the spiritual levels, at least we could cultivate a good heart.

Reflect on the Kindness of Everyone

The next slogan is, *Reflect on the kindness of everyone.* In other words, be grateful to everyone. If we train our minds to recognize the kindness of all beings, then despite physical discomforts, we shall always be joyful and happy, mentally and spiritually. Otherwise, we will suffer both physically and mentally. So we have to change our attitude. Self-cherishing is our true enemy to be annihilated, whereas sentient beings are our friends to love and to benefit as much as possible.

We shouldn't have gratitude only when people are being obviously kind to us; then we are grateful naturally. In other words, when people are doing what we would want them to do, of course we think they are nice people. But the real gratitude comes when people are not being nice to us, when people are not doing what we want them to do. When people are rude to us, are difficult to us, cheat us, lie to us, and even try to harm us—then too we need to be grateful.

Why? Because we need to cultivate patience, forbearance, tolerance, and the ability to feel great loving-kindness for *all* sentient beings. So, if people are always nice to us and act in the way we want them to act, although that is very lovely, we don't learn anything from it. It really is quite easy to be loving toward people who are lovable. We cannot develop patience toward people who don't strain our patience. The point is, when people are difficult toward us, instead of feeling angry, resentful, and upset by their behavior, we should feel a deep gratitude that they are being our helpers on the path to awakening.

Patience, forbearance, and tolerance are not signs of weakness; in fact, they are qualities of strength. Being angry and upset and irritable when people don't say or do what we want, that is weakness. Being a bully is weakness. Getting upset every time somebody says something we don't like, that is a weakness. But being tolerant and patient and conciliatory, that is a strength. It shows strength of character.

This patience, forbearance, and tolerance is one of the *paramitas,* one of the qualities essential for buddhahood. How are we going to develop it? One way is in retreat, sitting all by ourselves. That is very lovely. We can sit there radiating loving-kindness to all beings, because all beings are not there in our retreat. And then we go home, and what happened to our loving-kindness? What happened to our patience? What happened to our deep insights? We cannot develop them unless we have people who challenge us, who push our buttons.

So we should be grateful for the people we meet in our daily life, both the people who are nice to us and the people who are difficult—especially the people who are difficult, because they become our practice. *Thank you for being so obnoxious! Now I can really see where my mind is at.*

Please understand that this doesn't mean that we should allow others to harm us. That is not the point. Bodhisattvas do not behave like doormats, allowing others to step all over them. Out of concern for ourselves and others, we can stand our ground in a skillful way. The point is that the energy driving our actions is that of compassion and not anger.

The Self-Cherishing Mind Is Our True Enemy to Be Annihilated

In some versions of *The Seven-Point Mind-Training,* Geshe Chekawa says, *The self-cherishing mind is our true enemy to be annihilated.* Although this is not included in the translation of the root text that we are mainly drawing on, nevertheless it is an important slogan and appears in many other translations, so we will discuss it.

Sentient beings are our friends to love and benefit as much as possible. All sentient beings, not just nice, friendly sentient beings. It doesn't specify which sentient beings. As Shantideva and all the great masters have said, when people are difficult, people are challenging to us, this is when we should feel grateful to them, because they are helping us. They are helping us to develop the qualities needed to respond skillfully in difficult situations.

We might be wondering, "What kind of Dharma practitioner am I? Has the Dharma done anything to my mind in all these years, or am I reacting with the same old push-button reactions? How can we know where we're at in our spiritual practice if we don't have someone to test us?" This is how we are going to learn. As they say, now we can see our self-cherishing: We get upset when people are not nice to us. Why? It is because they hurt "me," they assaulted "me," they didn't do what "I" wanted them to do, they are trying to cheat "me." So it is this "me" that is the enemy, not the other person.

Otherwise, it is easy to get lulled into thinking we are much more advanced than we are. Very easy. Then we fall flat on our faces, and again we blame others. Our life always has challenges, so instead of thinking that daily life is the obstacle to our practice, we have to understand daily life *is* the practice. It is where we learn all those qualities needed for the path: generosity, patience, ethics, enthusiasm, and being mindful in the midst of chaos. And from that grows wisdom, understanding, and clarity. If we can be mindful and calm and peaceful only in calm, quiet, peaceful places and we get completely distracted in the midst of the bazaar, what use is our practice? No use. We take our mind with us everywhere.

The Buddha said that, wherever we go, we should keep a cave-and-forest mind. This means we should keep that same inner calmness, centered and mindful, and maintain that same kind of clarity of mind under all circumstances. The way we can learn that is not just by doing long retreats, but by sometimes being in the midst of all the external hustle and bustle and still keeping the inner clarity.

In this way, the mind does not go up and down. If people are kind to us, if people are cruel to us, it is the same. They are just sentient beings caught in the prison house of samsara. So, whether people are kind or cruel, we have compassion, we have empathy. We don't take it personally. We understand that, when people do bad things, not only are they creating very negative karma for themselves, but also there are causes and conditions for their being like that. Would we want their mind? So instead of feeling upset and angry, we just feel loving-kindness and compassion: *May you be well and happy. May you be free from suffering.*

By Meditating on Delusive Appearances As the Four Embodiments, Emptiness Becomes the Best Protection

The next slogan is, *By meditating on delusive appearances as the four embodiments, emptiness becomes the best protection.* The five poisons are, by nature, empty.* The five poisons in Buddhism are the root afflictive emotions that cloud the mind, cause suffering, and perpetuate samsara. They are:

Ignorance (or delusion): Not seeing reality as it truly is; misunderstanding the nature of self and phenomena. Ignorance is considered the root poison from which the others arise.

Attachment (or desire, craving): Clinging to pleasure, possessions, people, or experiences. Attachment causes dissatisfaction and grasping.

Aversion (or anger, hatred): Pushing away what is unpleasant. Aversion includes irritation, rage, and ill will.

Pride (or arrogance): Inflated self-view; considering oneself superior or inferior to others.

Jealousy (or envy, competition): Resentment of others' success or good fortune.

In Vajrayana Buddhism, these poisons are seen as not only obstacles but energies that can be transformed into the five wisdoms of enlightenment. For example, attachment transforms

* In Buddhist literature, the poisons can be divided different ways: Some works state there are three poisons, as mentioned earlier, while others state there are five or even six.

into discriminating wisdom, and aversion becomes mirrorlike wisdom.

When strong emotions come up—strong anger, strong passion, strong jealousy, any of these feelings—they arise in our mind. Instead of getting carried away by them, we look at them. Who is the agent of these poisons and the various thoughts and emotions they give rise to? Who is thinking this? Who is feeling this? And if we say, "I am," we are back to questioning, "Who am I?" And also, "What do these emotions look like? What does anger look like? What do jealousy and greed look like?" Look straight at them, nakedly. But if we analyze, we cannot find them. This non-finding, this absence, is the unborn dharmakaya.

Dharmakaya is the ultimate form of the Buddha, in the sense that it is the ultimate nature of the mind. It is all-pervading because all of nature is intelligent. Every cell of our body is intelligent. We are not just materialistic automatons. Every little cell of our body knows what to do. We don't have to tell it, thank goodness. It just manages perfectly well. There is an all-pervading intelligence here; it is not a person. The universe, the whole cosmos is intelligence. That innate intelligence is the dharmakaya. The whole cosmos knows what to do.

This is the unborn dharmakaya. It is unborn because there is never a time when it was not; we cannot say "before the dharmakaya." Dharmakaya is just what is. It is the nature of reality. So it is unborn, and it is also deathless because it is outside of time. Time—past, present, future—is a construct of the conceptual mind, and dharmakaya is beyond all that. Remember that, although everything is empty, it is not vacuous like empty space. It has intelligence.

Happiness and suffering and all sorts of feelings and perceptions arise endlessly, like reflected images in the mind. This reflection or appearance is called the *nirmanakaya*. That is the form that the buddhas and bodhisattvas take so we can see them. The mind's radiance and luminous quality is the *sambhogakaya*. Resting the mind in unborn, unceasing, timeless awareness is the protection of emptiness, which removes all confusion.

Dilgo Khyentse Rinpoche said the dharmakaya is like a totally pure, almost invisible crystal. We cannot see it because it is so clear. Then, if we shine a light through it, it radiates rainbows of the five colors. So that is the sambhogakaya. But the sambhogakaya is also the apparitional bodies of the buddhas and bodhisattvas on a high level, like Tara and Manjushri, that ordinary people like us cannot perceive. We have to also be on a high spiritual level to be able to perceive them. So, out of compassion, they then radiate down even further into what looks like an ordinary, embodied person that we can see.

For example, the Dalai Lama is regarded as an emanation of Avalokiteshvara, the bodhisattva of compassion, because ordinary people cannot see Avalokiteshvara in his sambhogakaya aspect. Out of compassion, Avalokiteshvara emanates as many beings, not just high lamas like the Dalai Lama and the Karmapa, but also ordinary sentient beings, and not just humans, but also animals and fish. Ordinary people can actually be emanations of bodhisattvas, who appear in many forms, in many countries, in many different guises in order to benefit other beings.

So these are the three kayas. From an experiential point of view, the nirmanakaya is the physical form; the sambhogakaya is the lucid and clear aspect of our mind; and the dharmakaya is the empty nature of the mind. The fourth embodiment, *svabhavikakaya,* is the empty, natural purity of the basic space of reality that exists outside of our perceptions. When all these come together, then the empty nature, the unborn, ceaseless, timeless awareness becomes the protection of shunyata that removes all confusion.

The Best Strategy Is to Have Four Practices

The next slogan is, *The best strategy is to have four practices.* These practices are accumulation, purification, generosity, and making offerings. These are very useful.

Accumulating Merit

One of the reasons why we experience so many problems and difficulties in our practice is because, from a Buddhist perspective at least, we lack the positive karma or the merit to clear away obstacles. It's like taking a trip: If we have money, we can stay in nice hotels and fly in business class and be comfortable, and we can travel easily with no problems. In fact, if we are rich enough, we just go VIP and don't even have to wait in the customs line. Whereas if we are poor, we then have to fly economy class, then take an ordinary old bus, bumping up and down, and maybe stay in the most awful kinds of hotels. So we experience many problems and difficulties while traveling.

In the same way, for some people Dharma practice goes very smoothly. They meet the right people at the right time; they get the right practices. When they practice, experiences arise. Everything seems to go so smoothly for them. Everything opens up for them as they need it.

Other people, even with great sincerity, have so many problems. They just missed the lama. He left yesterday, and he is not coming back for three months. When they try to practice, they have so many obstacles. They get sick, they have pain—so many problems, one after the other.

From a Buddhist perspective, if everything goes smoothly, it is because of the merit that we have accumulated—our good karma. If things are difficult in our practices—we just don't meet with the right situation at the right time, and we keep losing out—that is because of a lack of merit. Therefore, in order to create the opportunity to meet with these auspicious circumstances and for things to go smoothly so that we can continue on the path, the first practice is the accumulation of merit.

Merit can be accumulated in many ways: through generosity, through making offerings, through meditating on bodhichitta. Meditation on bodhichitta is a meritorious action because we are thinking of other beings and their welfare. We are aspiring to be of benefit and service to all beings. So this is a meritorious way of cultivating our mind.

Also of merit are meditations on ultimate reality, on the nature of the mind, on emptiness. Making offerings, being generous to people, doing prostrations, going on pilgrimage, making prayers of aspiration—all these create positive imprints on our mind stream. In this way we cultivate positive imprints, which in shorthand is called merit. So it means creating positive, good karma by doing good things and cultivating the mind in the right direction. So that is the first practice.

Purification

The second of the four practices is purification. We may have a lot of problems not only because we lack merit, but maybe we have demerits. So we need to clear them, to clean up. There are a lot of obscurations that need to be rubbed clean. In the Tibetan system there are many practices for this, such as the Vajrasattva practice of the hundred-syllable mantra; prostrations with the Thirty-Five Confession Buddhas; and Nyungne, which is a fasting ritual based on the one-thousand-armed Avalokiteshvara.

We can also use the Four Powers of purification: the power of reliance, remorse, resolution, and remedial action. The power of reliance—for example, simply relying on the Vajrasattva practice or Avalokiteshvara and so forth—helps to purify past unwholesome actions. Then there is the power of remorse: If we did something wrong, we must sincerely regret it. We cannot purify if in the back of the mind we are thinking, "That was not very good, but it was kind of clever. And I nearly got away with it—ha!" That attitude doesn't purify anything. So first we have to really regret. Then we resolve not to do it again. We really make a strong vow that in the future we will try to avoid those kinds of actions. And last, we find some kind of antidote, doing the opposite of whatever unskillful action we did before.

The main aspiration is that we are really sorry for everything that we have done that has harmed others—not only what we remember but what we don't remember—and we have the aspiration to clear this. We have the intention to purify so that we can practice properly and avoid the kind of obstacles that occur on the path, like missing the teacher, getting sick just when we are supposed to be practicing, and so forth.

Generosity

The third of the four practices is generosity. Generosity is considered one of the key virtues in Buddhism and serves as the foundation of Buddhist practice. Generosity is not simply about giving away material things. It encompasses the spirit of offering with an open heart, free from attachment or expectation of return. Generosity purifies the mind, counteracting the ego's self-centered tendencies. When we give, we break the habitual grasping and clinging that often defines our lives, allowing us to cultivate a deeper sense of compassion and selflessness.

Generosity can take many forms, including giving time, energy, knowledge, and love. The true essence of generosity lies in the motivation behind the act: the intention to benefit others without any desire for recognition or reward. This aligns with the Buddhist understanding that generosity helps to reduce attachment, which leads to greater freedom from suffering. By training ourselves to give without expecting anything in return, we build a strong foundation for further growth and create the conditions for cultivating other virtues, such as patience, ethics, and wisdom.

Making Offerings

The fourth practice is making offerings to harmful spirits with love and compassion. The practice of *chö,* which is popular among Tibetans, is one form this practice can take. Our nuns perform a short version of chö every evening, plus a three-hour chö practice every month. It was started in Tibet by a great *yogini* called Machig Labdron, who was a contemporary of Milarepa.

Basically it is a visualization in which we remove our consciousness from the body and we become Vajrayogini. Then we visualize our body, and we cut off the top of our head, which becomes a vast *kapala*, or skull cup. Then we visualize cutting up our body and throwing it into the kapala to cook, transmuting the impure body into nectar. We invite all the buddhas and bodhisattvas to partake of the nectar, and then we summon all the spirits to come. The text says, "If you're in a hurry, you can eat it raw. Or if you have patience, just sit, and it will cook." Supposing the ghosts and ghoulies really come and eat me? It is a way of facing our demons.

We have to visualize that we are having a party. Himalayan people believe strongly in the existence of all these spirits, and this is supposed to be practiced in a charnel ground at night. But of course the nuns are doing it in a temple hall. Still, we are inviting all these spirits to come. With joy! *Chö* means "cutting off," and we are cutting off our ego. We are cutting off our attachment to and identification with the body as well as our fear. We are feeding the spirits our ego and saying, "Eat up, and may you be well and happy. May all your bad karma be cleared!"

Chö is performed with a double-sided drum called a *damaru* and a bell. The liturgy is sung with nice tunes, so it sounds very pleasant. It is like a picnic, and everybody sings to the rhythmic sound of the drum and the bell. Everybody is invited to come to the party: Buddhas and bodhisattvas, lineage lamas, yidams, and all the spirits and demons, come and enjoy the feast!

This is a powerful practice in all lineages. The lineage of Machig Labdron died out, but the practice was taken by the other traditions. In Tibet, there were people called *chöpas* who would wander around Tibet and perform chö in the various charnel grounds. People would invite them to come to their homes or nomad tents because the chöpas had become especially skillful in clearing away sickness. Naturally they were on good terms with all the evil spirits who cause sickness. So then, if anyone was sick, the chöpas would be invited to come and perform chö in order to appease the evil spirits so that they would leave. Also when people died, they would perform chö, then also give offerings to the Dharma protectors, which are given on a daily basis, usually in the evening.

Whatever You Encounter, Immediately Apply It to Meditation

The next slogan is, *Whatever you encounter, immediately apply it to meditation.* In other words, utilize every immediate circumstance for meditation training. Whether in solitude or in the midst of the crowd, under all circumstances, favorable or not, maintain an equanimous attitude of utilizing all these situations as a help on the path to liberation. This means whatever we are meeting in this moment, we utilize it as our meditation. It is not that we meditate only when we are on our cushion or in a meditation retreat. We bring the mind of meditation to everything.

So what we are doing is accustoming the mind to being one with the Dharma in all situations. We practice so that, whatever we meet, our mind is stable and able to see things clearly, without distraction. There is a sense of clarity and space within our mind, so that we are calmly aware and we can respond appropriately. Whether we are in solitude or whether we are in a crowd, it makes no difference.

The mind should remain in a state of spacious attention and awareness. This is important, because usually we are doing formal Dharma practice for such a short period of time. The time when we are dealing with other people, dealing with circumstances, and living our ordinary life is so comparatively vast that, if we don't bring the two together, nothing will change.

So we have to stay mindful. Mindfulness, or awareness, is like yeast. If we think of ordinary, everyday life as a piece of heavy dough, then when we mix yeast with it, the mixture rises and becomes light enough to bake. We cannot make bread without yeast, but we cannot make bread with just yeast either. The two together is just right.

The quality of open awareness is essential. That is the yeast. We mix it with everyday life, which then lightens up. So it is important to have that quality of presence under all circumstances. This is what we are cultivating. In our meditation we cultivate it, then we practice bringing that awareness to daily life again and again, until eventually it becomes natural.

When I first started practicing, our togden yogis in Tashi Jong said, "Every hour you should make the commitment to look at your mind three times." That means whatever you are doing—walking, talking, working on the computer, whatever—instead of looking out there, go inward for a few seconds. In this moment, what is your mind doing? We are not judging it, just observing it. Every hour we can look at our mind three times, again and again. Gradually we become accustomed to looking. And gradually those moments of awareness get longer. Then awareness arises without our even thinking about it. Suddenly, especially in challenging situations, we become completely awake.

It is like anything: practice, practice, practice. We start with small things, and then the momentum begins to accumulate and build up, until finally—as it says here—everything that we meet is an opportunity for practice.

Obviously we cannot make the commitment that from now on, I am going to practice every second of the day. That is not feasible for most of us. We would disappoint ourselves because it's too difficult and then give up. But, if we set ourselves achievable goals, small steps, then we can build on those. We find that we can do it.

For example, one can commit to being conscious and present while cleaning one's teeth or drinking tea. They can make the strong determination: *Whenever I clean my teeth, I am going to do it without thinking of ten thousand other things. I'm going to just clean my teeth and be present with cleaning the teeth.*

We can all do that. And then we can extend it to another action and another action. Gradually the mind begins to get into the practice. We cannot say, for twenty-four hours a day, while we are sleeping and waking, we are going to be in a state of primordial awareness. But we can say: *Yes, when I drink a cup of tea, I'm going to really try to just drink the tea, taste the tea. I'm not just going to think about it or think about everything else except the tea.* We can make that commitment. Then we get confidence: *Yes, that was not so difficult. Now what else can I do?*

This is the point. We have to really start training to make our daily life our practice. Small but determined steps, over and over. Patience and persistence. Otherwise nothing changes.

4

THE FOURTH POINT

A Synthesis of Practice for One Life

Now we come to the fourth point.

To Synthesize the Essence of This Practical Guidance, Apply Yourself to the Five Powers

The first slogan in the fourth point says, *To synthesize the essence of this practical guidance, apply yourself to the five powers.* The Five Powers are resolution, familiarization, positive seeds, revulsion, and aspiration.

The Five Powers: Resolution

The first is the power of resolution, which really means a sense of throwing forward or making a resolution. It is the power of resolving that, from now until enlightenment, we will never abandon bodhichitta. This means, when emotional afflictions or *kleshas* come up, we will immediately deal with them. How we deal with them is up to us, but we won't just let them take over.

This power of resolution is very important. We need a sense of commitment to the path, that through all the ups and downs and the times when nothing seems to be happening, or even when we seem to be going backward, nonetheless we keep this inner sense of strength and resolution that we will not just give up or go off and do something else. We are committed, and we are never going to give up our aspirations for both absolute and relative bodhichitta.

This is important because that strength of resolution creates big imprints in our mind stream so that, not only in this lifetime but also in future lifetimes, we will again come back and meet with this same Dharma. This resolution is presumably the reason there are many people in the present time who have a sincere interest in Buddhadharma even though they do not belong to countries or cultures that talk much about bodhichitta.

The point is, because of past-life resolutions, in this lifetime, despite outwardly taking birth so far from this way of thinking and this kind of aspiration, causes and conditions have nonetheless been working together underneath it all to reconnect us with the teaching whose resolution we previously took. For some of us, maybe the teaching will be just a passing interest and we will go onto another track. However, for many people the Buddhadharma has already become a great commitment for their life, and so it is important not to give up.

Samsara is notoriously difficult, so this path takes inner strength and courage. It might look sometimes as if these lojong teachings are about being passive or giving in and not making a stand for anything. But there is only giving in as far as accommodating the well-being of others. Inwardly, it involves great strength and courage.

The Tibetan term for bodhisattva, *jangchub sempa,* was translated as "spiritual heroes," because there is nothing weak and wimpy about being a bodhisattva. We require this inner strength so that no matter what difficulties we meet on the path, whatever problems we have to face, we have the determination to keep going and not let anything stand in our way. We hold the conviction that this is the most important thing we can do: to develop the relative and the ultimate bodhichitta and devote our lives to this path.

Therefore, Chekawa says, this is the essence of all the instructions. The first power is our resolution that we will stand firm and not waver in our conviction that this work is important for all our lives.

The Five Powers: Familiarization

The second power is familiarization. In Tibetan, *gom* means to become familiar with something, and the word we translate as "meditation" is *gompa.* So meditation is when we become familiar with a practice because we repeat it again and again. It means getting the mind accustomed to new ideas, new ways of acting, new ways of looking at things. The power of familiarization means we become accustomed to the twofold bodhichitta under all circumstances. Lojong becomes second nature and feels natural.

At first, when we apply so many of these antidotes, it feels artificial. We repeat the aphorisms to ourselves, but we don't really believe it. This is simply because it is a new way of looking at things. It is a new way of dealing with circumstances and a whole new way of relating to ourselves and others; so it feels unfamiliar, quite alien. But any habit is formed merely by doing something again and again until it becomes second nature. And allowing the bodhichitta aspiration to become second nature is very important, because it is so closely aligned to our first nature!

We talk about how being angry or jealous is all second nature to us, an inherent state of emotion we experience. But what is our *first* nature? Forget the second nature. Our first nature is pure and perfect; it is buddha nature. So, if we make our bodhichitta into our second nature, then that immediately allies with our first nature. Then first and second levels merge powerfully, coming from the true source.

This familiarization is important. Repeating again and again until it becomes spontaneous—this is the essence of the practice. It becomes who we are, and we don't have to think about it. If somebody is irritating us or angry toward us, instead of getting upset and defensive and angry back, we can spontaneously recognize the poison mind that they are acting from. This will feel so sad, and naturally we will feel understanding and be patient and compassionate, not because we're trying to, but just because we see their state of mind intuitively and clearly. And our own state of mind too.

If we find ourselves getting upset and angry with all the defilements arising, then instead of beating ourselves up or being heavily judgmental, again tremendous compassion can arise. We will recognize these are not happy states of mind; these are not states of mind that bring us peace and clarity. And so the natural response will be a genuine sense of compassion for that and the wish to bring ourselves into more wholesome states of mind.

So, whether it is directed at others or toward our own inner pain, our response is not more anger, more frustration, more irritation, but instead deep compassion and understanding that then manifests as tolerance and forbearance. Because, what is there to be upset about? This response comes through familiarization. It comes through practicing again and again until it becomes natural to act in that way.

The Five Powers: Positive Seeds

The third power is that of the positive seeds. The "power of the white positive seeds" is part of the power of remedial action (one of the Four Powers of purification, which we discussed in the previous chapter). It involves intentionally planting and nourishing positive karmic seeds to:

> Counterbalance or purify negative karmic seeds.
> Shift one's momentum toward awakening.
> Strengthen virtuous tendencies in the mind.

In practice, this means to cultivate the seeds of bodhichitta and merit through constant reinforcement. Practice skillful thoughts, moment to moment, until enlightenment. Again, it is a matter of using our daily life to be always planting good seeds in our mind stream. Not just when we are in Dharma centers, not just when we are meditating or studying, but all the time we should be conscious of what thoughts are in our minds and deal with them.

The Buddha said there are four right efforts: First, there is the effort to eradicate negative thoughts like our greed and aggression, our jealousies and envies, and all these other irritations and self-centered types of thoughts. We need to recognize them and to pull them out like weeds. Then there is the effort to prevent those kinds of thoughts from coming in the future. Along with that, there is the effort to cultivate the good seeds, the goodness that spontaneously comes into our hearts, like thoughts of kindness, generosity, caring, compassion. And last is the effort to encourage their flourishing in the future. We cannot do any of that until we become more conscious of what is actually going on in our mind, at the time when it is going on.

So often, if we are in a bad mood or under the influence of heavy emotions, it takes time before we even recognize what is happening. We start getting angry and speaking sharply to people or reaching out and eating things that we know we shouldn't be eating, or whatever.

People nurture resentments—it is interesting how we nurture memories and thoughts that have caused so much hurt to ourselves, whereas the perpetrators have long since forgotten about it. However, often the goodness that people have done to us, we forget. So we recall all the bad things, building up this resentment, sometimes over years and years. Human beings are funny creatures, because we cause hurt to ourselves in ways like this. We think we want to be happy, and yet so often we do things that are going to result in our suffering. It doesn't help us, and it doesn't help others. Therefore, it is important for us to watch what is going on in our mind most of the day, because we are always talking to ourselves. So what are we talking about?

Imagine that the voice in our mind was a companion's voice instead. Would we want to travel with this person who is always nagging us and criticizing us and putting us down? Who has unrealistic expectations of us, telling us how we are supposed to be? I mean, what kind of companion is that?

The good news is, we can change the channel in our mind. Even neuroscientists are saying so now. People used to think, "Oh well, I've always been angry like this," or "I've always been very greedy," or "I've always been naturally self-deprecating." And, "It's my nature, and that's it. It's in my genes, I can't do anything about that. People just have to put up with it." But now scientists have discovered that this is not true; we might have certain characteristics, but it can all be changed if we make skillful effort.

Imagine our brain like a forest, and we normally take this trail because we went that way when we were young. It is familiar and has worn into a quite major road, easy to get through. Any alternative routes are full of undergrowth, so it's difficult to go another way. But we do know that our usual path has lots of snakes and leeches and nasty things, and it is actually not a nice pathway at all. In fact, if we go that way we are likely to run into danger.

So at some point we determine to go on another path. In the beginning it is difficult, because we are not used to that path, and in fact it is not yet a pathway at all. We have to make a new path for ourselves. But if we keep going that route, gradually it becomes a smooth trail. Meantime the old route starts to crumble, and all the weeds are coming up and taking over; soon it is not even used as a pathway anymore. The new pathway has become the familiar route.

The wonderful thing that neuroscientists in modern times have found out is that this is exactly what happens in the brain. They have labeled this as neuroplasticity. Normally, the impulses go down the neural pathways in the brain that they are accustomed to travel. Somebody annoys me, and I get mad. I always did this as a child, and nobody ever taught me another response. But, with the powers of familiarization and resolution, we can make new neural pathways in the brain. This is good news.

Scientists have found that, even in a few weeks of doing loving-kindness meditations, that part of the brain that has to do with kindness starts to be activated, and the area connected with anger, low self-esteem, and depression becomes smaller. Once the brain is trained to go in a certain direction, it starts to create neural pathways in that new direction.

But we have to keep practicing. So it is important to be conscious during the day about messages we are giving to ourselves, which means becoming more conscious of what we are thinking. We need to start looking at and hearing those thoughts. When the messages are negative—when they are critical and heavily judgmental and just reworking the same old stuff again and again—we can look at that. We can analyze our thoughts and say, "No, that is not good, that is not helpful, that is not true. I am going to give myself new messages instead."

We can do it. We can start giving ourselves positive messages. We can start giving ourselves approval when we do something kind and good.

It is like in the garden. We have to pull out the weeds, but we also have to put fertilizer and water on the plants we want to grow. The Buddha always said that, although we should regret the negative things we say and do and think, we should also rejoice in the goodness inside us. Because if we don't, then like a plant that doesn't get any water, it will grow up spindly, even if it came from a good seed. So, just as we encourage others in their goodness, sometimes we also have to encourage ourselves.

This is not the same as feeding the self-cherishing mind. Self-cherishing means always thinking only about "me." This is about encouragement in the right direction. In order to walk the path until we are almost at the end, we have to take ourselves with us, so it makes sense to have a sense of self that is happy and content, that delights in wholesome thinking, in wholesome speech, in wholesome actions. Why? Because that sense of self isn't concerned with itself.

When we meet truly good people, they are usually thinking only about others—they have gotten themselves out of the way. People who have a lot of harsh thoughts in their heart, toward themselves or toward others, are always thinking about themselves because they are out of balance. So what we need is to get in balance. We need to change the recording that we are always playing in our head to a more positive and encouraging message, full of white thoughts.

There is an old Tibetan story about a certain *geshe*. *Geshe* in those days did not mean a scholar; it meant someone who was following the Kadampa school of Atisha. He decided his mind was a mess. So he sat next to a pile of black pebbles and a pile of white pebbles, and he just began looking at his mind. Every time he had a negative thought, he put aside a black pebble. Every time he had a good thought, he would put a white pebble.

In the beginning, of course, there were many black pebbles and very few white pebbles. But, as he became more conscious in this way, they evened out. Eventually he had only white pebbles.

This is a sweet little success story, but it also shows the geshe wasn't beating himself up when he had only black pebbles. He was just becoming more conscious of how many negative thoughts go on in the mind—not only directed at others but also directed at ourselves. This inhibits our ability to blossom, so it is not virtuous to be always beating oneself over the head, metaphorically speaking. When we see a negative thought, we apply an antidote, and then that turns it into a positive thought. And when our minds are filled with positive thoughts, we are happy.

When we are happy, we want to share our happiness with others, and we have the ability to share our happiness with others. When we meet great masters, they have so much inner joy. They don't have to do anything or say anything. Just being in their presence makes us feel better, because these masters are totally in balance.

So we have to start planting some nice, white seeds. We recognize the dark seeds and decide, "Those dark seeds are no use. I've lived with these dark seeds so long. They didn't make me happy, they didn't make other people happy, and they just created problems. So I am not going to cultivate dark, poisonous seeds. I am going to start cultivating nice, clean, white seeds to grow a beautiful bodhi tree in my heart."

The Five Powers: Revulsion

The fourth power is revulsion, or repudiation. This power is about getting really fed up with samsara and utterly repudiating the self-cherishing mind because it is the cause of all our problems. With this power we completely disown the ego.

"I am really fed up with this. I've been carrying along my self-concern throughout endless samsara. It is enough already. Always thinking, *me, me, me*. How to make *me* feel better. How to make everything work out so *I* feel okay. And, at the end of all my efforts to make *me* happy, I am just more miserable than ever. I am fed up."

That is the feeling: that we have really had it with always trying to make ourselves happy and giving in to all our egocentric desires. We recognize that this attitude doesn't work, doesn't bring happiness. If we don't recognize this, we will carry on always hoping that, if we just got more—more real relationships, more security, more possessions, more, more, more—somehow things would finally work out, and we would feel okay. But in fact that way of thinking is going in the opposite direction to where true happiness lies.

True happiness lies in really rejoicing in the happiness of others and not being so overly concerned with our own well-being. We are responsible to ourselves, but without that total absorption in our own benefit and lack of concern for others' happiness.

So at a certain point, we begin to see that we have been endlessly self-absorbed, even just in this lifetime, from when we were little babies up until now, and that it hasn't worked. We feel such a weariness. It is like carrying a backpack of heavy rocks on our back. Liberation is exactly like our putting down the rucksack of self-concern and just relaxing.

So it's an interesting balance, because on the one hand we are dealing with how to be more skillful with our mind, which is a self-concern, and yet at the same time we are cultivating how to drop the self-cherishing attitude and be there for others. But observing the mind is a useful self-concern. It is skillful to get our mind into balance, to train our mind so that we can function skillfully under all circumstances without thinking of ourselves the whole time. To act for the benefit of all beings, we have to find an inner balance within ourselves.

Nowadays many people seem to have everything that the television, movies, newspapers, and magazines assure us we require to reach happiness. Many people seem to have it all on a material level. So why do so many people suffer from depression and anxiety, if life with abundance is so great? In fact, this total self-absorption that is taught, especially nowadays, is just so tiring. It leaves everybody feeling so frustrated with their lives, which seem empty and meaningless. So there is the sense that we are on the wrong track. We really are weary of that. It is enough.

This is an important stage to reach, because otherwise, when things start to go better, our resolution begins to weaken. Maybe everything before hadn't been quite right, but this is really a good apartment. She is really a special woman; the other women, they were the cause of samsara. This one is the one. I didn't quite like my job before, but the new one really makes me happy.

So we really have to understand from the depths of our hearts that there is no genuine satisfaction in samsara. The reason is not the outer samsara but our inner samsara. That is the big problem. We have to turn the inner samsara into nirvana—that is the only way to do it. The only way for us to make that effort is to recognize what the problem is.

If we were very sick, if we didn't really believe we are sick, we would never undergo the course of treatment, especially if the course of treatment is quite painful. It is only when we understand that this medical treatment is our only chance to recover that we will agree to it. Likewise, spiritually speaking, we will suffer until we recognize the real problem, which is that we don't believe samsara is really as bad as the Dharma books say. In this sense, we are all sick and all in need of treatment. But we are not accepting that; there is still the hope that, somehow, we can manage and things will be quite nice. The basic insecurity and tight grip of our obsessive ego absorption is really not appreciated except when things are difficult. This means we don't really have renunciation.

Renunciation doesn't mean merely giving up things on the outer level; it means inwardly losing interest. We are all stuck here, because we haven't yet made this inward shift in attitude. Therefore, we must practice cultivating bodhichitta and making merit throughout the day, whenever circumstances arise. We work to cultivate bodhichitta, both ultimate and especially relative bodhichitta, under all circumstances, remembering we are here for the sake of all beings, to bring happiness and relief to all beings, not to create more problems for them.

Completely disowning the ego means that we just see it as it comes up and we don't necessarily listen to it. We recognize that it is just our ego. Sometimes it is good and helpful, and sometimes it will lead us into all sorts of problems.

The world is filled with all these hard egos fighting each other, each one thinking they are right. But we do not get rid of the ego by flagellating or starving it. Like someone with a donkey: If they beat the donkey, yes, it will go along, but they have a sad and broken donkey. That is not how we deal with the ego. If we beat the ego, criticize it continually, make it feel miserable and so forth, its humility will not be a genuine humility; it will just be a broken sense of self. But a broken sense of self is still a self.

So if we have the determination to really transform and change, and to replace what is negative in us with what is positive, we do that like a trainer with a good high-spirited horse. The trainer doesn't beat the horse but understands it and encourages it, soothing and cherishing it so that the horse wants to train, wants to do more than the horse had thought it could do.

People who have psychological problems are often the ones most absorbed in their ego, even if it is a very sad ego. Again, merely beating ourselves up is not going to help us open into the fullness of our wisdom and compassion mind. Someone said that true humility is the absence of anyone to be proud—no self to feel pride. There's no "I" thinking, "Oh, I'm ever so humble." Genuine humility is just that, because we are not thinking about our self, we are thinking about others. Everyone we meet is the most important person in our life at that moment because that is the person we are with. We are not wondering what they think about us, because our ego has stepped out of the way; we are looking at them only. Then the heart opens to embrace all beings. But the heart can do that only from a well-balanced sense of self that is at peace with itself, working on itself in a way that is kind and good—not in a way that is judgmental and harsh. With compassion. So bodhichitta is very important.

The Buddha always said that when we do loving-kindness and compassion meditations, we start with ourselves, because we are the first in need of loving-kindness and compassion. When we feel that gentleness and understanding toward ourselves, even though we are striving to overcome our defects and cultivate our virtues, it is a happy task. It is not like a cruel schoolmaster standing there with his stick, waiting to beat anybody who gets out of line. We don't need a heavy taskmaster inside our mind. We are suffusing our mind with compassion and understanding and acceptance, because then we can give all those good feelings to others.

If we are harsh and judgmental toward ourselves, we are harsh and judgmental to others. So, while we are on the spiritual path, when we are really practicing to recognize and transform or apply antidotes to our negative emotions and to cultivate and encourage our positive emotions, we do this out of love and compassion. Not like a dogmatic schoolmaster. We don't do virtuous actions out of fear or out of disgust with ourselves, but because we recognize that, by acting in this way, we are coming back to our true nature. Then we will feel much better. And we will be able to make others feel much better also.

In this way we have to work with our mind skillfully, not creating more problems but just recognizing. When a negative feeling comes up, we recognize it. Some people say we should name it: anger, jealousy, greed. So we accept this is the feeling that is coming up in our mind right now: "I'm angry," "I'm irritable," "I'm jealous." We accept this is the thought that came up. *This is what I am feeling right now.*

So then what do we do? Well, let us not pour more oil on the fire. Let's apply an antidote. There are various ways of dealing with negative emotions. For instance, we can replace the emotion with a positive emotion. Or we can look at it very clearly and see that it is just like a bubble. Emotions have no solidity. We can listen to what they are telling us with a friendly attitude. But again, until we recognize the emotion, and until we recognize there is a problem, we will not even look for the solution.

Learning all of this requires the Five Powers. It requires resolution, the power of familiarization, the power of positive seeds, the power of revulsion or repudiation. And, as we begin to learn about our own mind, we also begin to understand the minds of others—not just from reading books and taking courses but by observing ourselves. We are all quite similar, really.

The Five Powers: Aspiration

The fifth and final power is that of aspirational prayer: the direct wish to evolve and become more beneficial. In Buddhism in general and in Mahayana Buddhism in particular, *monlams*, or prayers of aspiration, are important. We are not praying for more money, a better relationship, or long life—those are just worldly prayers. Examples of aspirational prayers are: *May I truly cultivate the twofold bodhichitta. May I live my life to be of real benefit to other beings. May I realize the nature of the mind. May my life be truly meaningful for others as well as for myself. May all beings be well and happy and free from suffering.*

Aspirations—whatever inspires us—lift the mind. We can make our aspirations to ourselves, but we can also make those aspirations to all the buddhas and bodhisattvas of the universe. For example, if one is a scholar, then one will make one's aspiration prayers to Manjushri, who is the bodhisattva of wisdom.

Many people make aspiration prayers to Tara because she is a very active lady. She is usually shown with one leg coming down off her seat, meaning that she's ready to get up and do something immediately. She is not just sitting in deep samadhi. So she is a great bodhisattva to whom to direct prayers of aspiration.

In any case, the important thing is the sense of lifting up the heart in aspiration to fulfill one's real motivations. It helps us to clarify what we really want, especially in a spiritual sense. Aspirations are mostly dealing with spiritual matters.

In the Mahayana tradition the universe is filled with buddhas and bodhisattvas. The idea is that this universe is filled with light and love and intelligence, which in the Buddhist tradition we call the buddhas and bodhisattvas. Their function in this world is to help us. They do not judge us, and they certainly are not there to punish us. They are totally on our side. Their aspiration for us is that we may fulfill our own deep inner aspirations. As far as possible, they will help. Prayer in any religion is always an important part of the spiritual process.

Sometimes people say, "Oh, I prayed and prayed, but it didn't happen." But the point is, maybe it wasn't meant to happen. There are many reasons for this. One may be that it could not happen at that time because of karma. Second, maybe it is better that it didn't happen. We have to remind ourselves that reality is like a vast, endless tapestry. We don't see the whole pattern. We see such a tiny piece of that tapestry, this small part. If one bit has lots of dark threads woven into the design, it might seem like an ugly pattern to us, and we might want some more bright colors in there. But, if we could stand back and look at the whole picture, we'd see the dark lines are an integral part of the whole design.

It cannot be all just bright colors. There have to be dark colors in there too. It could be that these higher intelligences such as the bodhisattvas see the whole pattern, and so they recognize that we have to go through this darkness. It may be an important part of our spiritual journey. In these cases they don't interfere, because they have not only compassion but also wisdom.

We can aspire, we can pray, but in the end we have to accept. We have to accept it is just the karmic patterning that we have created. It will happen as it is going to happen. If it can be changed to our liking, then that is fine. The most important thing is that we don't pray for just mundane benefits.

For example, many people come to me and say, "I need a teacher." Well, they can pray and make aspirations to find guidance. If it is possible, if the karma is there, then it may well happen. It is not that they will meet some teacher seated on a thousand-petaled lotus radiating lights, but they might meet an ordinary-seeming person who can show them the next part of the way.

Aspiration lifts up our hearts and reminds us of our own potential. Prayers of aspiration are beautiful; they lift us up from our ordinary, mundane preoccupations, to thinking of something beyond ourselves and reflecting back to us our true potential. In the Mahayana there are many prayers of aspiration. But we can also make up our own that speaks to our heart. The important thing is that it should touch and uplift our heart.

Lift up our hearts! That is what we have to do. Through the power of aspiration, we encourage and remind ourselves to cultivate the qualities that we need in our life and our practice.

The Mahayana Teaching on Transferring Consciousness Is Precisely These Five Powers, So Your Conduct Is Crucial

The next slogan is, *The Mahayana teaching on transferring consciousness is precisely these five powers, so your conduct is crucial.* This is concerned with what to do at the time of death using the Five Powers. In the Tibetan tradition there is a practice for the time of death called *phowa,* where one ejects the very subtle consciousness (which is conceived as residing in the center of the chest) out through the top of the head. This avoids entering into the bardo, or intermediary state, and instead the consciousness goes into higher realms.

Incidentally, some people practice phowa in preparation. The sign of success is that the top of the cranium opens up and a blade of *kusha* grass can be inserted into it. So, when people are practicing phowa, they are all walking around with kusha grass waving out of a small hole in their head! Even my mother did it, so it is not just for advanced yogis. But we won't discuss that practice further.

Here we have the Five Powers again but in a somewhat different order and now dealing with the time of death. The change in order is due to the change in context. At the time of death, or transferring consciousness, things are very different from when we are fully alive: All our senses are dissolving, and our capacity for this kind of practice is different.

The first power when approaching the time of death is the power of positive seeds. We need to give up all attachment to this life and give away to others our possessions and our wealth. It is important that, as we get nearer to death, strong grasping and clinging should not arise. We should completely drop all attachment. Because our first attachment is often to our wealth and possessions, we should give everything away beforehand. Let other people enjoy. We can take nothing with us except the seeds of our own actions, so we might as well enjoy giving them away first. That is called the power of positive seeds.

Next is the power of aspiration. That means we make aspirations to meet with the Dharma, bodhichitta, and spiritual masters in future lifetimes. We can also confess any faults that we have, aspire toward goodness, and dedicate all our virtues to others. It is important at the time of death to really aspire to meet again with the Dharma and have faith. We can think, "I'm really sorry for all the wrong I've done, but I aspire now to all the goodness that I'm capable of. Please in my future lives may I always meet with a spiritual guide." It is important to think like that at the time of death.

The next one is the power of repudiation. Recognize that the primary cause of spinning on the wheel of samsara is our grasping at our self and our wealth, relatives, and friends. This clinging is our greatest enemy. It doesn't mean we cannot love others. Love is a wonderful quality of heart. Love is not the problem. The problem is grasping and clinging, which causes suffering. So we cultivate the feeling in our heart that we will let go and not grasp and cling.

As we are dying, often friends will come and our relatives will be all around crying, "Don't leave us, don't leave us!" This is not helpful. It is much better, if they want to be with us when we are dying, that they should sit quietly, maybe say some prayers or just quietly do tonglen. Perhaps they can gently remind us of all the goodness we have done in our life. On the other hand, if one is sitting with a dying person, you can tell them to think of whomever they have faith in. If they are Buddhist, they can concentrate on whichever Buddha or Bodhisattva or teacher they have devotion toward. Or if they are Christians, to focus on Jesus or the Virgin Mary. Get them to think of that object of devotion. Lift the mind up toward them. If they don't have any particular faith, then they bring their mind toward the light. It's best not to encourage people at this stage to think about their objects of attachment, family and friends, their nice house, or their favorite cat. This is not the time; they are leaving that now.

The same applies to ourselves during the death process.

Then there is the power of resolution. In the past we cultivated bodhichitta, and now it is important to maintain and apply this at the time of death and during the bardo. Again, we must think, "What was my spiritual practice? I must take that with me, especially the twofold bodhichitta and all my aspirations and my devotion to the various higher beings and to the teacher. All that I will take with me. In the bardo, in the intermediary state, and in future lives, may I always spontaneously practice what I have learned in this life." We make that resolution that we will do that. We are not going to forget and get distracted in the bardo. We are going to know where we are going, and we will use that time to cultivate even more and more of these spiritual qualities.

Last is the power of acquaintance or familiarization. While maintaining acquaintance with bodhichitta, we lie on our right side with the cheek supported by the right palm and the ring or little finger closing the right nostril. As we breathe, we visualize giving and taking, the tonglen meditation on love and compassion. Compassion is breathing in all others' sadness, and love is breathing out all one's buddha-like qualities. That is one thing that anybody can do.

If one is more advanced than that, they can meditate on emptiness by reflecting that the true nature of all that exists is empty of substance and self-existence; it is illusory, like a magic show. If one has had definitive experience and realizations of emptiness, then this is the time to meditate on how nothing has substantial existence, everything comes together with causes and conditions, and so forth. Or, if one has realized the nature of the mind, then of course they will rest in the nature of the mind, in pure, primordial awareness. Depending on our level of attainment at the time of death, that is how we should practice.

Generally speaking, it's not good to die in a hospital. We don't want people racing around, sticking tubes into us, and moving us around or whatever. At that time what we need is peace and quiet. The people around us need to be quietly meditating or gently chanting prayers. We need the opportunity to get our mind calm and centered and be able to bring our practice to fruition at this very important transition point. As much as possible, it is much better for people, if they truly are dying, to be left quietly with no more than a few quiet presences there. We need space to center our mind and do our practice, because whatever state of mind we take into the next stage will be very decisive for our future.

It is also important that, if we are sitting with somebody who is dying, we don't disturb them. Perhaps we just quietly play a recording of some prayers that are appropriate for them. Or we can quietly chant mantras, if that is what they want. Basically, we allow them to have the time and space to make their transition peacefully and in an appropriate frame of mind, because what is in their mind at the moment of death will likely influence their future. This is an important point. We really should cultivate how to be with the dead and the dying in a way that truly benefits them as well as benefits us.

We should not think that death is the ultimate failure, as so many doctors do nowadays. Of course, it is not a failure at all; it is perfectly natural. Just as we welcome birth, we can welcome death. We have already died so many times before—no big deal. But it is important to recognize that we should set up good conditions for people to help make their death a good transition.

If the dying person has fear, we must assure them that there is nothing to fear. We can remind them to think of the light, go toward the light. Don't fear the light.

5

THE FIFTH POINT

The Criterion of Proficiency in the Mind-Training

We are now up to the fifth point, which is the presentation of having trained the mind. Now, the Buddha gave eighty-four thousand different teachings, but all of them are to help us do essentially one thing: subdue our ego clinging. This means we need to analyze whether the practice of the Dharma is actually reducing our self-cherishing mind, or if we are still caught up in the eight worldly concerns. This section deals with a way for us to check whether the Dharma is actually working or not.

The Whole of Dharma Is Synthesized in One Aim

The first slogan under this point, *The whole of Dharma is synthesized in one aim,* is a reminder that the Dharma that was taught by the Buddha is really intended to subdue and overcome our ego obsession, our self-concern. Again, is our practice actually doing this, or is it caught up in what are called the eight worldly concerns, which are gain and loss, praise and blame, good reputation and bad reputation, and pleasure and pain? If we think of it, so much of what we do in our lives involves exactly these concerns—gaining something or dealing with loss, seeking praise or giving blame, worrying about our reputation, and underlying it all, seeking pleasure and avoiding pain.

If we are practicing hoping that somehow our Dharma practice will bring us more gain and praise, that we will get a good reputation, and that all this will bring us even mundane happiness, then we are caught. Because along with those comes the other side of the coin: loss and criticism, disrepute and painful experiences.

Each side has its flipside. If we go for hope, we experience fear. If we go for gain, there is the risk of loss. If we go for people praising us, they might also criticize. If we care one way or the other—if our mind hasn't the equanimity to deal with gain and loss as just two sides of the same coin—then we suffer. We can't avoid worldly circumstances: People sometimes praise, sometimes they censure; sometimes we have a good reputation, but then somebody spreads rumors; sometimes things are pleasurable, other times everything goes wrong and life is painful. How are we responding in all those changing circumstances? That is the question.

It is that our underlying motivation that counts. If we are still practicing in order to gain the rosy side of that duality and to avoid the more difficult, dark side, then we are still caught up in the samsaric motivations of the ego. However much we practice, we are still just practicing in the orbit of our self-concern. Our practice is not reducing the ego, it is polishing the ego—a nice, shiny ego. This is something we have to be careful of. We have to ask ourselves: Why are we really practicing?

Attend to the Chief of Two Witnesses

With the next slogan, Geshe Chekawa mentions another way of assessing whether we are on the right track: *Attend to the chief of two witnesses.* What others think or say about us is one witness. But this witness cannot see our thoughts and intentions, so the principal witness is ourselves. We should look honestly at our own faults and virtues. We should live up to our own precepts to avoid becoming the object of our own scorn.

The secondary way, public opinion, can be right, but it can also be disastrously wrong. People whom others hold up as exemplary may end up having clay feet; even if they are fine people, there is always someone wanting to bring them down. On the other hand, we can look honestly at ourselves. Looking honestly means not just looking at all our faults, either, because they are not the full picture. Along with all our faults, to make a just assessment, we also have to look at our virtues and pure motivations.

Sometimes people think that being honest with ourselves means looking only at the worst about ourselves and not appreciating the goodness. Then we become depressed and downhearted. That is not what it means. We simply have to make a fair assessment, like that geshe with his black stones and his white stones. In the beginning, yes, there were a lot of black stones, but he didn't get depressed. He just kept working on his mind until eventually the stones evened out, then finally there were no more black stones.

We don't have to be harsh judges, but we need to be honest in our assessment of ourselves. What is wrong with us? That is our practice. That is what we are working on. If we were all perfect, we wouldn't need the Dharma path. We would have already made it. It is because we have imperfections, but we also have aspiration to deal with them skillfully, that we are walking the path. The path is there to help us deal with our weaknesses and faults and transform them into strengths.

Like going to a gymnasium to work on our weak legs. We don't say, "Oh, my legs are so weak—no use going to a gym." We go to the gym *because* we have weak legs. And then we exercise to have strong legs. But at the same time, we don't forget that, even though we might have weak legs, our arms are quite strong. So we also keep exercising our arms too, but with the emphasis on those legs.

All of us have weaknesses. All of us have problems and frailties. Of course we do. If we think we don't, then we are really in trouble. But if we magnify those faults to the exclusion of what is good and right within us, then we are being unfair—just as if we judged another this way, only looking at their faults and never seeing anything good in them. That would be unbalanced.

The text is saying to witness honestly, so we can see both things that need to be dealt with and also the strengths we already possess that can help to enhance our practice. We are the only ones who can see what is going on inside us, so when we look inside, we should be an honest, unbiased witness.

Constantly Resort Solely to a Sense of Well-Being

The next slogan is, *Constantly resort solely to a sense of well-being*. It is easy to be cheerful when things go well, but the test of our genuine practice is our attitude in the face of adverse circumstances. Lojong encourages and trains us to be cheerful whatever happens. This is important because sometimes lojong sounds very grim—all this bashing away at self-cherishing mind. It sounds like every time we fancy an ice cream on a hot day, we scold ourselves and think of all the people who don't have any ice cream. But that is not what is intended, so it is good to be reminded that it is good to be cheerful under all circumstances.

Again, it is easy to feel joyful when things go right, but how do we respond when things go wrong? We must practice to sustain that inner joy and to be more even-minded. Of course, it doesn't mean that if we suffer the great loss of someone we love, we should go around saying, "Never mind, death is for everybody. It's all impermanent." That would be monstrous and totally unreal. If one loses someone one loves, one grieves. But even so, the grief should not go on forever, and our sadness should be blended with Dharma reflections and the pure aspiration that this person who died should go to higher realms. We should do what we can to help through prayers and dedication of merit. Meanwhile, the acceptance of death happens. We see grief is not just happening to me; it is happening all over the world, every minute. That is the nature of birth and death.

How someone responds to things that happen depends on their own inner state, so even in our grief we can feel some inner assurance and understanding as we take that experience onto the path. Practicing gives an inner sense of well-being, even in the face of life's tragedies, during which, as Dharma practitioners, we should look and see whether we are responding in the same way as if we had never heard a word of Dharma. Or has something inside us genuinely shifted so that now we are on a boat riding the waves of samsara and not quite so immersed and tossed around by those waves?

So yes, be cheerful. When one meets great Dharma practitioners, they are usually happy even in very demanding circumstances. Buddhas and bodhisattvas are shown smiling. It is not because they have their eyes closed to, or feel indifferent about, the sorrows of the world. Their eyes are open, their hearts are open, but they are still smiling.

If You Are Well Trained, You Can Practice Even While Distracted

This is another slogan not included in the particular translation of the root text we are using, but it appears in many other translations, so we will include it. The slogan is, *If you are well trained, you can practice even while distracted.* For example, experienced riders do not fall off their horses or their motorbikes. When we first start, if we are riding a bike or a horse, we are holding on tightly, trying to keep our balance and absolutely focused on what we are doing, so that we don't fall off. But, once we become accomplished in riding, whether a motorbike or a horse, then we can go along, relaxed and looking at the scenery, and we are not going to fall off. People can be talking to us, and there is a part of our attention that is focused on what we are doing, but we are not fearful of losing our balance.

Likewise, when harm or difficulties arise suddenly, if we maintain our equanimity, our loving awareness arises spontaneously, which shows we have some practice of lojong. It is easy to practice calmness in a retreat situation, but the real test is everyday life. This again brings up something that many people ask: Is it better for me to be in retreat or to stay with my family? Different people depend on different circumstances, but basically it is a matter of breathing in and breathing out. If we are always breathing in, we will asphyxiate. The same will happen if we are always breathing out. We need the rhythm. So, in addition to some retreats, our regular daily practice is helpful. Even if we only practice for half an hour a day, that is better than not practicing at all. This gives a sense of centeredness, especially if one practices in the early morning. Morning practice gives a sense of balance to help us cultivate awareness during the rest of the day.

The feeling of spacious inner balance has to be carried throughout our daily lives—with our families and our colleagues, in our workplace and our social life—because if we can only practice being equanimous when there are no distractions, then that is not true equanimity. Obviously, that equanimity would be very fragile. There should be a calm, clear, silent center. To attain that open awareness, first we need to do more practice. Then, once we have stabilized this sense of presence, we need to test it.

Again, it is somewhat easy to be friendly, cheerful, and loving when everything is fine, but when we meet with adverse circumstances what happens? Do we spontaneously respond with equanimity, love, and compassion? Or do we completely lose it and snap at everybody? Do we get upset or frazzled or stressed out?

If we do lose our balance, then okay, now we know. We failed that exam. We need to do a bit more study; it is not the end of the world. But now we know at what point we are likely to lose it. So then we go back and strengthen again and again until we finally can keep our balance. Then we know that something is actually changing inside.

If we were baby birds, just out of the egg with very few little feathers, that would not be the time to pretend to be an eagle. We are like featherless fledglings. We don't have to put ourselves to tasks that are too heavy right now. Nonetheless, we have to gradually gain strength until we can soar like eagles. Eagles can fly with the minimum of effort. Our mind should gradually become like that, just gliding in the vast, open space of *dharmadhatu,* but very clear and sharp. Those eagles are wide awake and looking at what is happening down below. It is the middle way between being too harsh and judgmental of ourselves and being too easygoing and condoning. It is not a matter of trying to gain anything, but we have to feel that our practice is going forward.

Sometimes people say, "Well, if I do all this darn practice, what will I get out of it?" That is not the point; that is just the ego speaking. Nonetheless, if we sincerely try to apply these precepts, something inside will change. It doesn't change in the sense of experiencing fantastic lights and visions, but in small ways. Something may happen that previously would have really upset us, but now we find it doesn't upset us, that inwardly we do have more stability. Progress is usually slow, but it is built to last.

6

THE SIXTH POINT

The Pledges of the Mind-Training

Now we come to the sixth point.

Always Abide by Three Principles

The first slogan here tells us, *Always abide by three principles.* These three principles are as follows:

> Keep the three levels of vows
> Avoid being ostentatious
> Avoid being biased

The first principle—to carefully observe the three levels of vows—means observing, with the intention to benefit others, the Shravakayana precepts, such as the refuge in the Three Jewels and the five ethical precepts; the Mahayana bodhisattva vows; and the Vajrayana tantric vows. We should be careful when observing our vows. Each of these vows has many subvows, like the forty-eight bodhisattva vows and so forth.

The second principle—to avoid being ostentatious—means not using our Dharma practices to impress other people with our virtues or our levels of realization. In other words, avoid engaging in flamboyant behavior, such as imitating the *Mahasiddhas* and thinking of yourself as a great yogi or yogini. It is very unnecessary and could be harmful. It is much better to be authentic and modest in behavior.

Basically, this means not to make a big display of our practice, that we should be secret practitioners in a way. Unless we are monastics, we don't need to wear certain clothing or look a certain way. When I first became Buddhist in London when I was eighteen, I didn't know any other Buddhists. I had just read a single book on Buddhism, but I knew I was a Buddhist. The book I read talked a lot about renunciation. So I thought, *Yes, I must renounce.*

The first thing I renounced was Elvis Presley (this was in the early 1960s). That was the hardest. I gave away all my rock 'n' roll records. Then I gave up whatever boyfriend I had at that time. I gave up my clothes because I thought, as a Buddhist, I should dress simply. My poor mother—she made me these kind of Greek tunics in yellow, which I wore along with black stockings. I gave up all my other clothes and I told her to give them away. I didn't wear makeup. I wore flat shoes. Now I was a Buddhist. People would ask, "Do all Buddhists look like you?" I couldn't answer them. I wasn't sure what Buddhists looked like because I'd never met one.

Eventually, after some months, I decided I needed to meet some more Buddhists. So I looked them up in the phone book. The only center I could find was the Buddhist Society, which was in London. The president was an English judge named Christopher Humphries. I went there, and nobody else was wearing Greek tunics. They were wearing ordinary clothes. Some of them were even wearing makeup and high heels. I thought, *Oh, maybe I made a mistake.* I had missed something somewhere. Then I said to my mother that it was a pity I had given away all my clothes. So she handed me the key to my wardrobe, and there were all my clothes. My mother was very skillful.

The point is not to be ostentatiously showing that we are on a spiritual path. Actually, I wasn't acting out of the desire to be different. The book said to renounce, so I was trying to renounce everything that I held dear. But still, it was foolish. The point is that, while we are practicing, we don't have to look particularly like we are practicing. We just act normally. The transformation is inward. It doesn't have to be outward.

The third common principle is not being biased. The commentary explains, "Some people are polite to powerful people and disdainful toward the poor and weak." That is one interpretation of being biased—how some people are all charm and politeness toward the big patrons. We see it in monasteries that go out of their way for the big sponsors. Ordinary people who can only offer a few rupees tend to get ignored and shoved into the corner. Sometimes in certain places, if you are a wealthy sponsor, you can get to meet the teacher. If you are just an ordinary person, there is no way. So the third principle is to not be like that, but try to be open to everybody. Rich or poor, powerful or weak—it doesn't matter. They are human beings who need help. If we can help, we help. If not, at least we can be polite.

Another commentary says that being biased is being friendly to relatives and friends and hostile to strangers. Again, this is about not favoring one group of people and being disdainful of other people. It means not to be partial or prejudiced, to have love and compassion for all sentient beings, irrespective of gender or race or class or nationality or anything. We are all sentient beings and equally in need of love and compassion. We shouldn't make a lot of distinctions between people in that way.

Shift Your Priorities but Stay As You Are

Then the text says, *Shift your priorities but stay as you are.* Again, this is about being honest and not being ostentatious in our conduct. While we strive to correct our inner attitudes, the actions of our body and speech should blend with that of others. That doesn't mean that if we go to a social gathering and everybody is getting drunk, we have to get drunk too. What it does mean is that, even in that case, one shouldn't be ostentatiously abstaining. We can refuse the alcohol gracefully and drink mineral water. We don't have to say, "Oh, no thank you—I took a vow from His Holiness the Karmapa never to take alcohol because we know that alcohol is the root of all evils." We won't be invited back.

We can quietly abstain from doing a lot of things without making a big issue of it. When I was in Italy once, I got sick and I was in the hospital. It was a big hospital in Perugia. I explained that I was vegetarian, and they all looked at me like I was from Mars. Then the chief cook turned up, and he asked, "Why are you a vegetarian?" My Italian not being good, I said the simplest thing I could think of. I quoted George Bernard Shaw: "Animals are my friends, and I don't eat my friends." After that the cook made delicious vegetarian food for me. The whole ward was full of envy! The point is, I didn't need to give him a whole lecture on the evils of eating meat. It doesn't mean he became a vegetarian, but maybe he went away and thought about it. And nobody was offended.

It is important that, even when dealing with people who don't hold the same kind of views as us or have the same kind of conduct, we can be true to our own convictions without making a big song and dance about it. Quietly and unostentatiously, we can hold to our own principles. We are not missionaries. We don't have to have everybody conforming to our own views. We teach more by our conduct than by forcing everybody else to follow our lead.

Therefore, the changes are inner changes. But our outer actions and speech should blend quietly with others. Our outer behavior remains constant, and the inner transformation grows. It is a mistake to make great outer displays of change, especially when inside we have changed only a little bit. That becomes hypocrisy: "Oh, now I'm a Buddhist, so I have to make these big outer changes, yet inside, same old mind—only now it has some Sanskrit terms in it!"

Finding Refuge

The entrance onto the Buddhist path is to take refuge. Refuge is the foundation for all Buddhist practice, including lojong. Technically, it should be discussed with the preliminaries, but this is also a good place to discuss it, because many of the slogans that follow could be said to flow out of the refuge commitment as well as the five fundamental Buddhist precepts. Many people are sincerely practicing the Buddhist path, yet they have never taken refuge. They are not quite sure why they should. This is a little bit like saying you are a Christian, but you have never been baptized. In Buddhism, taking refuge in the Three Jewels is regarded as opening the door to the Buddhist teaching. It is an affirmation of our confidence in the Buddha, his teaching, and his enlightened followers.

It is a simple ceremony that has been performed much the same way since the time of the Buddha. The Buddha would meet someone, he would talk with them, and then he'd give them some teaching. At the end of the encounter, they would then recite: "From now on until life's end, I take refuge in the Buddha, I take refuge in the Dharma, I take refuge in the Sangha." Right from the earliest days with the Buddha himself, this was the formula. It is still used in all Buddhist countries. It states that one has confidence in the Buddha as a teacher, in the teaching as the truth, and in the community of who have practiced and realized this truth.

The Buddha sometimes is compared to a physician, because we are all sick. We are poisoned by our greed, anger, delusion, pride, and jealousy. These poisons that create so much pain in our mind stream and cause so much trouble in the outer world. So the Buddha is therefore the doctor who gives the medicine. The medicine is the Dharma. The Sangha are like the nurses who help us to take our treatment.

When we take refuge in the Buddha, first we take refuge in Shakyamuni Buddha, because without him there would be no Buddhadharma at all. We also take refuge in the Buddha in the sense of all the buddhas and bodhisattvas of the universe—the intelligence, love, and luminosity of the universe. Furthermore, we take refuge in our own innate buddha nature—the genuine buddhahood of wisdom and compassion that is within ourselves. We take refuge in that because our ultimate refuge is our own wisdom nature.

The Dharma represents the teachings of the Buddha as preserved in 108 volumes of what he actually said. *Dharma* also means the truth—how things really are when seen with unclouded vision. The Dharma points to how things really are, not how we see them through the lenses of our own dualistic delusion.

The Sangha represents, first of all, the monastic sanghas of monks and nuns. It also means the great fourfold community, which is ordained monks, nuns, laymen, and laywomen. All the followers of the Buddha are considered the *mahasangha*. It also means the *arya sangha*, the noble sangha. That means anyone, whether ordained or lay, who has actually had an experience of the truth, who has actually had an experience of the nature of the mind or nirvana. So they know firsthand, and therefore they are a refuge for us too.

The actual ceremony is very simple. It confirms our adherence to the path. In essence, it says, *Right now I am truly committed to this path. I am not going to look around at all these other paths. This is going to be my path.* Meanwhile, I have taken precepts in Tibetan, Chinese, Korean, Vietnamese, Sanskrit, and Pali, and so it is a relief to hear the refuge ceremony in English, because at least I know what we are saying!

The Five Precepts

Along with refuge, we can also take the five precepts. These five precepts are the basic precepts in all Buddhist schools. They are not concerned with what we wear or what we eat. They are solely concerned with living in this world harmlessly so that, even if we don't do much good, at least we don't do any harm. They are based on the perfect conduct of an *arhat*, who has become egoless and realized nirvana. An enlightened being would naturally, spontaneously never commit any of the faults that are enumerated in the precepts.

The first precept is not to take any life. That of course means not to kill. But it does not just mean human beings; it means all beings: animals, fish, birds, insects, anything that has consciousness. We take the vow—why? Because even an ant holds its own life as most dear. It has its own meaningful life. We don't know how an ant feels. It certainly is a being with its own feelings and its own agenda in life, and however long it may live, that is a fulfilling life if we happen to be an ant. What right have we to deprive that being of its life?

We would not like some alien from outer space to come and look at us and think, "Oh, what funny two-legged beings," and then crush us! We would resent it. Likewise, we should be careful with the lives of other beings. If we tap the surface next to an ant, it would turn and run away because it senses danger. It knows that something nearby is threatening. We are all the same. Even an ant has buddha nature. It might take time to realize it, but all beings have primordial consciousness. Therefore, we vow not to intentionally take the life of any other being.

The second precept is not to take that which is not given—that is, not to take the property of other beings, meaning not to steal. This also means that when we borrow something we should give it back—books, tapes, DVDs. These things do not get legs and run off by themselves. They are given a little help. We should be scrupulous when we borrow something from someone. We should treat it carefully, better than we would treat our own possessions. We give it back in at least as good condition as we received it.

The third precept is the precept against sexual misconduct. That means that, since the sexual urge is such a strong one, we should be wholly responsible for our sexuality, that we should not use others purely for our own indulgence. Instead, we should be very careful and responsible not to create any kind of harm, either to the person, to ourselves, or to others who might be in any way involved in the relationship. It's about being responsible for our sexuality and treating this in an adult way, instead of just using it as a means of sensual gratification.

The fourth precept is concerned with speech. Our speech should not only be truthful, it should also be kind, helpful, and nondivisive. Some people enjoy saying things that pit one of their friends against another. This is harmful speech. Our speech should be nonslanderous, nonabusive, nondivisive, and truthful. We should abstain from useless, meaningless talk and gossip. That will shut most people up.

The fifth precept is against intoxication. It is to abstain from any alcohol or drugs that distort the mind, because in Buddhism the mind is the most important thing. Therefore, we do not want to do anything that will cause us to lose control over the awareness and mindfulness that we are seeking to cultivate. Many people do terrible things under the influence of drugs and alcohol that they would not do when they were sober. Therefore, this is the precept to abstain from inebriation and remain clearheaded.

If there is any precept that one feels one cannot keep at the moment, then that can be omitted. In the refuge ceremony we can keep silent during that part. Of course, it is much better discipline to take precepts that are difficult and challenging. But, if we feel we cannot observe one yet, then we can just leave it for now.

The Bodhisattva Vow

Then, there is the bodhisattva vow. Again, there is an elaborate ceremony for the bodhisattva vow, separate from the refuge ceremony. There is also a simple alternative. The simple one is mainly repeating certain verses from Shantideva's *Bodhicharyavatara*. Again, if we are taking the bodhisattva vows, it is good to do so in English so we know what we are saying. It is helpful to understand them, because otherwise we cannot put forth a heartfelt conviction.

When we take the bodhisattva vow, it doesn't mean that afterward we immediately become first-level bodhisattvas. It is a vow of aspiration to strive for our own enlightenment in order to liberate all others—however long it takes! There are two levels of the vow. First is the aspiration. Then comes the determination to commit to a bodhisattva's way of life as best we can.

None of these vows are commandments. There is no Buddha up there with a lightning fork about to spear us if we break any of them. The precepts of nonkilling and so forth are described as rules of training. We are trying to conform our conduct to the spontaneous behavior of an enlightened being, that is all. Likewise, in the bodhisattva vow, we are going to seriously commit ourselves to trying to follow the way of the bodhisattvas.

So we read books on the bodhisattvas' conduct, like the *Bodhicharyavatara* by Shantideva and others. We study the meaning of bodhichitta. We study books that explain to us about the forty-eight vows of a bodhisattva. It is not that anything horrible is going to happen if we get upset or angry or whatever, but it is reminding our inner self that now we are getting serious about this bodhisattva path. Now we are really going to commit ourselves to the discipline of training and transformation. This is a key that opens the Dharma door. We may not have entered and explored everything in there yet, but the door is open now. We can go in.

Therefore, the bodhisattva vow is something momentous in our spiritual journey, and we can receive it again and again from as many great teachers as possible. It is not that we take it once, and then that's it. We can receive the vow again and again. Each time we take the bodhisattva vows, or the precepts or refuge, they are embedded in our mind stream, so that in the next life we will come back and definitely find the bodhisattva path again. Therefore, whenever we have the opportunity to take these vows, we should definitely do so.

Do Not Speak of Others' Limitations

The next slogan is, *Do not speak of others' limitations.* This means not criticizing or finding fault with others' physical or mental defects. We should not talk to others about someone's handicaps. If somebody has some kind of disability or mental challenge or so forth, we do not need to point this out to others. Certain low-minded people may mock and joke about others' defects. Obviously, we would not do that, and nowadays on the whole, people are more sensitive.

So, recognizing that these things are not important, we don't criticize or find fault with people's defects, either in front of them or behind their back, just as we wouldn't want everybody discussing ours and pointing their finger. Nowadays, most of us would not do that anyway. It is a childish mind that delights in laughing at other people's difficulties and defects.

Do Not Stand in Judgment of Others

The next slogan is, *Do not stand in judgment of others.* Finding faults in others merely reflects the impurities of our own minds. It is better to think positively about other people rather than ponder their inadequacies. When we look in the mirror of other people, we see a dirty face because our own face is dirty.

This again has to be understood. It doesn't mean that we become completely naive and stupid. If people are cheats and rogues, we should be conscious that they are cheats and rogues. If people are doing things that create much harm to others, we should be conscious that they are harmful to others and do what we can to prevent that. However, what this does mean is that it's easy to see others' faults and then say lots of negative things. It is easy to talk about them—"Oh, she seems nice, but have you noticed . . ."—and get pleasure from discussing the faults and flaws of other beings. This habit is demeaning to others, and it just illustrates the antagonism in our own mind, the flaws of our own mind.

In Vajrayana Buddhism we talk a lot about pure perception. Pure vision or pure perception means regarding all beings as deities. It is especially focused on the root guru, the lama, that if we see faults in them, that is merely a reflection of our own inadequacies. This can also be quite dangerous. But here, it is not coming from a tantric point of view. It is dealing with the situation from an ordinary, everyday perspective: If we endlessly find faults in others, maybe the problem is not the others. The problem lies in ourselves. Why is our mind so critical? Maybe they have those faults, but so what? If they are not serious faults, we don't need to discuss them all the time.

Sometimes there are people who highlight the faults of whomsoever they meet, and the goodness in others is overlooked and does not get any attention. We all know people who are endlessly telling us all the gossip and scandal and all the things that people have done and why they shouldn't have done it. This happens often in families. It happens in relationships: What is not so good in the other person is magnified, and all their good qualities diminish. People don't regard what is pleasing in their partner or appreciate what they are doing right, because their attention is totally focused on what is wrong.

If we find ourselves being constantly critical and always seeing the faults in others, then there is something wrong with us. That we are so critical, so skeptical, is a symptom of a problem in our own mind. It is a reflection of our own inner aggression and aversion. It is like looking in a mirror. What we see is not the fault of the mirror; it is not the fault of the reflection. The mirror is just reflecting our own face.

Again, we have to have discernment and common sense—we can't be totally naive and allowing others to take advantage—but on the whole, we should be careful not to be endlessly looking for and thinking about faults in other people. We should aspire to seek out their goodness.

Of course, the antidote to our own critical thoughts is the application of the lojong slogans, the very things we are learning now. We can pause, connect with the breath, and repeat the slogans.

Whatever Mental Affliction Is Strongest, Purify That First

In some versions of *The Seven-Point Mind-Training*, the next slogan is, *Whatever mental affliction is strongest, purify that first.* We have many afflictive emotions. Almost everybody has some kind of anger, greed, jealousy, pride, and so forth to cope with. This is what it is to be an ordinary sentient being. We all have some faults. In fact, if we really look, we probably have a lot to deal with. Among all those afflictive emotions, there is bound to be one that is especially difficult for us. That is the one we should focus on first.

Again, it is like going to a gymnasium. We work on the whole body but concentrate on our weaknesses. It is exactly like that. Yes, we have to look at the whole picture, but in particular, we have to assess our weakest point. What is the problem that causes us to fall down again and again? We all have afflictions, but people differ in their specific problems. Find out what our worst fault is and concentrate on dealing with that. In this way we build up the skill and courage to deal with the lesser defilements.

If we are not sure what our particular weakness is, we could ask our friends. Then we read books, we listen to talks, and we really reflect on the antidotes to this particular problem. Then we work on it. We are careful to see when this particular affliction arises and how we are dealing with it. Is our response skillful or unskillful? Are the antidotes that we are applying actually working or not working at all? And so forth. We have to be serious about this.

The path is recognizing and dealing with all our afflictions, but it is difficult to take on the whole plethora of all our faults.

So it is helpful to single out the most pressing one for particular attention. We work on that one and recognize that as the path. This is how we advance. Do not try to bypass a fault, thinking it will cure itself as we become more advanced. Usually the afflictive emotion will just stay with us as an underlying condition. So we need to face it, right at the start. We could even name it and say, "Okay, you and I will have a little relationship here. It's time that something changes, and it's going to be you."

Abandon All Hope of Reward

With the next slogan Geshe Chekawa is giving advice on how to take these practices onto the path: *Abandon all hope of reward.* Because we are working to develop bodhichitta *for the benefit of all sentient beings,* our practice is impure if we aim for only our own personal gratification and reward. Meditating and practicing with an ambitious mind is just worldly activity. Therefore, we should practice free from personal hopes and fears about the result.

Sometimes people practice because they think it will make them feel happy. But actually, in the beginning it could make them feel worse. In meditation practice, for example, as we go below the surface waves of the chattering mind, our awareness begins to sink down into the vast ocean of the mind, and we can meet with all sorts of strange beings—beautiful fish and monsters of the deep.

At the same time, we might stir up a lot of the mud and the garbage at the bottom that may start to surface. So again, we may very well feel worse instead of better for some time. If we hope that the result of our practice is that we are going to feel so much better—calm and blissful, loving and compassionate under all circumstances, and so forth—we will be discouraged. It might be that the exact opposite happens: We become more upset, more irritable, more prone to ups and downs. But this is only temporary. For a long time, positive results may not be noticeable because this is a practice of gradual, inner transformation, and for now it is happening at a deep level that we cannot actually see.

But everybody's mind is different, so our experiences will therefore be different. Some people work for years and years and nothing seems to change, then suddenly everything changes for no obvious reason. Others, presumably because of practices in past lives, quickly attain high levels of understanding. We cannot know what to expect. Scholars have created wonderful gradations on the path, but maybe that is a scholastic fantasy. Everybody is different, so the challenges that we meet are going to be different too.

Therefore, it is important not to make arbitrary assessments: "Oh, I've been practicing years and years, and I haven't had a single vision—it must mean I'm not doing it right." We cannot judge. It is difficult to judge for ourselves. But the general idea is that we can feel when things are getting a bit better. We may feel a kind of inner equanimity and joy. We may become less critical of others. When things go wrong, we can summon up a certain inner equanimity and understanding to help us through difficult times. We don't completely fall on our faces.

These are not dramatic realizations, nor are they just small insights that fade in the light of day. They are subtle changes that can permeate our inner being. Therefore, we should not be looking for results. Wanting to get something, to gain something, is part of our mundane life. We want to succeed, but the spiritual path is not like that. On the path, we are actually deconstructing, not building up. We are deconstructing our whole approach to who we are. So that takes time, and it takes skill, and we don't know exactly how it will all turn out in the end. It will be beneficial, but there are no hard-and-fast rules.

Regardless, in the books they often give us signposts—this is going to happen, that is going to happen—when in fact there are no guarantees as to what we will experience, because we are all different. Nowadays our modern psychology is different from the ancient psyche; the way our minds work is not the same as in the past. Our experience—what arises for us as the result of practice—is likely to be different from the signposts described in the old texts. Either way, don't stop to look for results. Just keep going.

Avoid Poisonous Food

The next slogan is, *Avoid poisonous food*. The poison here is ego clinging, which can contaminate all our spiritual activities and turn their nectar into poison. So keep in mind the four thoughts that turn the mind away from samsara: remembering the precious human birth, karma and rebirth, impermanence and death, and the wretched state of samsara. Also keep in mind bodhichitta and the inherent emptiness of all things. These contemplations help to keep the mind on track.

As the text says, wholesome deeds performed with selfish aims are just like poisoned food. So, as much as possible, we should try to do our actions with the motivation of bodhichitta and the basic understanding of *shunyata*, or emptiness, not just for the gratification of our own ego. Even our best actions are contaminated by the wrong motivation: "I'm being generous because then everyone will think I'm such a nice person."

It is nice to be generous, but it is better to be generous out of a joy in giving rather than because we want people to admire us. In the Buddhist world, laypeople are especially concerned with gaining merit or positive karma. Therefore, many Asians, even ordinary people without a lot of wealth, are extraordinarily generous. Many of them choose to remain quite anonymous; they just delight in being generous. But sometimes, especially among the wealthier, they want to gain a reputation for being generous: "They are such wonderful sponsors! They are so special! They constructed this whole monastery!" Then they feel so pleased with themselves. This is contaminated action because, although the action is good, the motivation is mixed with self-concern, with the self-cherishing mind. Then it becomes like a poison.

One time the Buddha was invited to lunch with his monks at the home of a wealthy merchant who was a big donor. There were many delicious dishes, and the servants were all dressed up. The neighbors were invited to come and look on, so as to admire this big sponsor's generosity and glory. At the end of the meal, the Buddha said, "To whom shall I dedicate the merit?" So the merchant said, "Well, to that one who is most deserving of the merit."

The Buddha turned toward the doorway, where there was a beggar woman looking in. The woman had been thinking, "Isn't it wonderful that this sponsor has given so much good food to the Buddha and all his monks! I'm so happy for him. It's wonderful that he's making so much merit like this." The Buddha said, "The one who gained the most merit was this beggar woman, because her motivation was completely pure, which yours is not." Then the Buddha dedicated all the merit to the beggar woman.

That is the point: Even wonderful actions like offering a huge banquet to the Buddha can be contaminated if they are done with an attitude of pride. So, even our best deeds, if done with a sense of our own self-promotion, become contaminated. Therefore, if we can manage it, we should do whatever we do with the motivation of compassion, love, and bodhichitta and with the underlying understanding of emptiness.

In generosity, there are said to be three cycles. If I think, "I am offering this flower to this person, and they are happy. They say, 'Oh look, she has given me a flower.' How nice. So we are all happy." But still the action is contaminated. It is contaminated in three ways: by the thought that I am giving something, by the idea that something is actually happening, and by my belief in an object and a person who is receiving it. In three ways we are caught in this reification again, making something seem real and solid.

So, although giving is a good thing to do, in itself it is not going to lead to awakening, because the idea of generosity is already trapped in three levels of delusion. If we recognize that ultimately nobody is giving anything to anybody, then we are okay. But as long as we grasp at the idea of an existent self who is doing a real action to another existent self, then generosity doesn't lead toward wisdom. Even a good action is contaminated by our wrong views.

Do Not Indulge in Self-Righteousness

The next slogan is, *Do not indulge in self-righteousness.* It could also be, *Do not be predictable.* Geshe Chekawa, in his commentary, says we should not refrain from condemning acts of injustice committed by others and that we shouldn't stop ourselves from holding them accountable out of a misplaced sense of loyalty. What does that mean? Perhaps it means to not keep quiet when someone we are attached to (or even devoted to, such as a guru) does something wrong, even though we know they are guilty—not to be silent in the face of wrongdoing, no matter who is doing it.

On the other hand, Dilgo Khyentse Rinpoche says it means not to be so faithful to our parents' or family members' memory that we inherit their obligations or pursue their vendettas—not to be ruled by such prejudices. Ringu Tulku says, do not repeat negative patterns over and over again. Do not nurture old grievances and grudges that fortify the ego.

For me, this one is about holding grudges, like in honor killings and these sorts of family and tribal rivalries. Some have always had these rivalries with other families, such as certain Scottish clans. They carry on with these vendettas, without any reason for it beyond the fact that this is what has always been done. Judgments and vendettas against people who haven't done anything to harm us are just prejudices that we have inherited. Importantly, nurturing old grievances and grudges only fortifies our sense of self.

Remember this text is from Tibet, where there are age-old tribal conflicts and sectarian rivalries that people have held on to throughout the centuries. They have nothing to do with anything now. But everywhere in the world, it is the same. People hold on to prejudices against other people, without having any personal reason for doing it. That hatred is nurtured across generations. So, if anybody in your family has been nurturing grievances and grudges against another family since childhood, please drop it. Moreover, if your social environment promotes notions of racism and bigotry, try your best to distance yourself from that and don't follow what the rest of society is doing if you recognize it as nonvirtuous.

Do Not Engage in Malicious Sarcasm

The next slogan is, *Do not engage in malicious sarcasm.* When someone ridicules and insults us, we should not retaliate by returning sarcasm and slander. Instead, we should practice patience. We should not utter a word that harms others or makes others unhappy.

This is an important one, especially in relationships. Very often people get into the habit of harsh speech toward one another. They are not even conscious of how harshly they speak to each other. So, if we find ourselves getting caught up in these kinds of patterns, we should definitely stop.

We may think that speech is harmless—"Sticks and stones may break my bones, but words can never harm me"—but that is not true. People are very much affected by speech. Many more people are harmed by harsh words than are harmed by physical abuse. Often people hold insulting words in their hearts forever. Therefore, we should not speak any hurtful words.

I had a friend who was an attractive and intelligent woman. She had a business and was very successful. She had a nice, goodhearted partner who really was extremely fond of her. But she constantly tried to break off any kind of relationship. Finally she realized it was because in her head she always heard her mother's voice from when she was young, saying, "Oh, you're so stupid. You're ugly, and nobody will ever love you."

Obviously, her mother was angry at the time, but those words replayed in my friend's heart over and over from that point on so that she grew up believing that she was ugly and stupid and unlovable. As a result she kept pushing away anyone who tried to get close to her and love her. She held the core belief that they couldn't love her; they must have some other reason they want to be with her because she was unlovable.

In this way many people hold in their hearts the harsh words, the abusive words, that have been said to them in their youth. It is the same later on in relationships. All the good words we forget, but the harsh words we hold. So this is important, not to become perpetrators of harsh speech. We cause so much harm by the unkind words we say, even when we don't really mean them—we just said them because we happened to be having a bad day, and so forth.

Lojong is about living in the world in a way that will both benefit others and help us overcome our self-clinging thoughts. Therefore, we have to really lock down our speech where anything negative is concerned, because somehow harsh talk sinks right down into the center of people's hearts and hurts them. It can destroy them, actually. This is an important thing to remember. Never speak harshly to others. If you feel like saying something insulting or critical or mean, just bite your tongue—especially in relationships, because giving some clever, biting answer that hurts the other person is never skillful.

Human beings are the only animals on this planet with the gift of formal language. Therefore, we should be incredibly careful what we do with this great gift.

Do Not Wait in Ambush

The next slogan is, *Do not wait in ambush.* Troops who cannot defeat their enemies in open combat often wait in ambush, using guerilla tactics to surprise and defeat their foes. We should not harbor vengeance for a harm done to us, waiting for the opportunity to retaliate. Relinquish all thoughts of revenge and stay peaceful. If someone harms us, we shouldn't nurse thoughts of revenge or bide our time, waiting until we finally cause them pain or even a downfall. If somebody has done something bad to us, we must let it go.

Do Not Strike at the Heart

The next slogan is, *Do not strike at the heart.* This is another one that is not in every commentary on Geshe Chekawa's root text but is nonetheless worth outlining. This slogan means we should avoid exposing another person's weaknesses, especially when others are around. Do not use spiteful words that penetrate another's most vulnerable point. Again, some people delight in pointing out someone else's vulnerable spot and causing them humiliation and pain. Obviously we should not do such a thing, so please don't do it.

Do Not Load the Burden of a Dzo on an Ox

The next one says, *Do not load the burden of a dzo on an ox*. Well, that is obvious. A *dzo* is a cross between a yak and a cow. They are very strong. What this is saying is don't load a person down with responsibilities or things to do that are beyond their abilities. It is like so many of these poor donkeys we see in India who are overloaded and eventually end up with broken backs and legs. We should avoid doing this, metaphorically speaking.

Also, we should avoid shifting blame and liability that should fall on us onto another person. Further, we should not accuse someone else of something in order to avoid the blame ourselves. This is especially bad when we blame someone who is in a weaker position and cannot defend themselves.

This is all about not exploiting people—not placing undue blame and not expecting anyone to do a task they are incapable of doing, thus making them feel bad and inferior.

This text was written in a culture where many people had servants and slaves. It is a reminder for the masters not to overburden their servants, to be fair toward them, and not to expect more than they are capable of giving.

Do Not Flatter Your Way to the Top

The next slogan is, *Do not flatter your way to the top*. We do not need to be the best. We can allow someone else to succeed. Being jealous of another's spiritual achievements or trying to outdo them does not help. This is not a race or a competition—an important point, especially in Dharma circles. Sometimes, people tend to see Dharma practice as a kind of competition: Who is going to win? Who is going to come out best? But this is not a race. We go along at our own pace; we don't have to look at what everybody else is doing.

We can see this in meditation retreats especially. Everybody is sitting there, and some people are looking to check how everyone else is doing. "Oh, they're all in samadhi, and I'm just sitting here with sore knees." We don't have to compare ourselves with anyone else. We are each unique and special, and we need to work on ourselves, not worry about what other people are doing. We don't have to outrace anybody else.

Avoid Pretense

The next slogan is, *Avoid pretense.* If we are devious and stray into manipulation or diplomacy to hide our real motivations, this shows we have forgotten the reason for our training. In other words, we should try to be as honest and straightforward as possible. We shouldn't be devious, try to manipulate people, or have ulterior motives.

We should be straightforward. We should be trustworthy. People should believe that we mean what we say. What we promise to do, we will do. We should be upright and act with integrity, because otherwise we have forgotten the reason for our training in the first place, which is to live for the benefit of others.

Do Not Bring a God Down to the Level of a Demon

And then the next slogan says, *Do not bring a god down to the level of a demon.* Lojong is about overcoming self-grasping. Therefore, we must avoid becoming inflated by its practice and generating conceited thoughts of being compassionate and so forth:

"Oh, I'm such a great bodhisattva." If our *kleshas,* our negative emotions, increase instead of our bodhichitta, then we have a problem. If we become proud—"Look, now I'm so patient, and I don't get angry. I must be at least a first-level bodhisattva by now!"—then we are bringing the god down to the level of a demon. So the advice is to always take the lowest place and consider ourselves the servants of all. Pride and jealousy turn the god of genuine bodhichitta into a demon.

We should, especially in small communities such as monasteries and Dharma centers, be conscious of that and try to bring everything onto the path and avoid making what looks like a perfect setting into a field for the growth of further defilements. We have to be careful that we really are using this opportunity to further our bodhichitta, not to further enhance our negative emotions, which is so easy to do. This is why we need to be constantly on the alert. That is why the lojong teachings say to take the lowest part and consider ourselves to be the servant of all. We shouldn't think that we are something special, that other people have to serve us. In this way the likelihood of this transformation from god to demon will not take place.

Do Not Take Advantage of Another's Misfortune

The next slogan is, *Do not take advantage of another's misfortune.* If we try to gain anything, even satisfaction, from the pain or the misfortunes of others, this is the total opposite of wishing them well and rejoicing in their happiness.

Remember, we have vowed to work for the happiness of *all* sentient beings, and that means all—even people whom perhaps we don't like. When Osama Bin Laden died, for example, there was rejoicing in his death, which is shameful. That is what this slogan is advising against. Rejoicing when misfortune comes to people we don't like, who have harmed us, or whom we perceive as our enemies is very negative. Again, to rejoice in anyone's pain and unhappiness is the absolute opposite of bodhichitta.

When we hear that somebody has done something terrible and is being punished for it, it is natural for us, in our delusion, to rejoice that the evildoer has gotten what they deserve. We should observe that and think, "Okay, this is the result of their own actions, but may they learn from this, and may they transform and become a better person in the future." It is not right to jump up and down with glee because somebody we don't like is suffering. Even in small things we should be careful of that. When something unpleasant happens to someone we don't like, rather than feel pleased, we should intentionally generate compassion and empathy.

7

THE SEVENTH POINT

The Precepts of the Mind-Training

We have arrived at the seventh and last section of *The Seven-Point Mind-Training.* In some texts this is called "Presentation of the Precepts of Mind-Training." This section is a summation of how we should act in order to bring lojong into our lives.

Synthesize All Meditative Practices in One

The first slogan reads, *Synthesize all meditative practices in one.* So what brings together everything we have discussed so far? What is the essence of what this lojong text is trying to say? We should act with compassion and pure motivation in everything we do. That is what it all comes down to.

Whatever action we take—eating, walking, working, sleeping—we should have only the motivation to benefit others. That is basically what lojong is about. Our whole life, no matter what we do and what ordinary actions we perform, we should undertake everything with this motivation that we may be of benefit to all beings. This compassionate motivation should be underlying everything we do. If we can cultivate that throughout each day in all our activities, then, when we are faced with challenges and difficulties, this attitude of patience and of compassion will arise spontaneously.

If we only expect right motivation to arise when difficulty comes, it will be too late. We have to practice this motivation in all activities, including those that are totally unchallenging, so that our mind becomes accustomed to it. Then, when we need it, it is already established because we have practiced.

Throughout the day we should cultivate awareness and compassion. Then all our activities, even very ordinary activities, become meaningful. This is another important point. There are no ordinary activities anymore. They are all the actions of a bodhisattva.

Someone once asked me about my teacher Khamtrul Rinpoche, "Why is it that when Rinpoche simply picks up a cup to drink, it has so much significance? Whereas for us, even when we do all the fancy things, it still doesn't have much meaning?" No matter what he did, it felt like you were watching a buddha—not because his actions were studied and grave, but because one could feel the underlying pristine awareness and compassion in every action. It was just natural, it just flowed.

All of us should try to practice like that, try the best we can to remember that we are now going to act, inwardly, as a bodhisattva. Outwardly we will look much the same. Even so, that motivation and aspiration will slowly permeate everything we do, just naturally. Otherwise, if we just try to be bodhisattva-like on special occasions or when we are being really challenged, it probably won't work. It will be too weak. We have to practice at all times to be aware and compassionate to the best of our ability—not just to others but also to ourselves. Compassion is for all sentient beings, and we are also a sentient being. We need to cultivate that attitude of kindness.

Respond in One Way to All Bouts of Dejection

The next slogan is, *Respond in one way to all bouts of dejection.* This means that when bad things happen to us—people hurting us, accidents befalling us, our negative emotions increasing, or a lack of interest in practice (which is a difficult one for many people)—we should think of all the beings in the world who are suffering likewise. How sad it all is. Even if we explain Dharma to them, they would not be interested. So we should wish that, on top of our own suffering, we could also take on their suffering. This is back to tonglen again, sending out loving-kindness and compassion.

Tonglen is the antidote to all our misfortunes. When something horrible happens to us, instead of getting completely engrossed in our own suffering, we try to realize how many other beings in the world are suffering likewise, or even worse. We also muster the sincere wish to take on all their sufferings at this time and for them to be free of their sufferings. Then that puts the whole situation into perspective.

When not-so-terrible things happen that upset me, I always think, if this were the worst thing that was happening in the world at this moment, then this would be a Pure Land. We have to have perspective. And, when we do come across great suffering, it is important to recognize that this is something that we share with so much of the world. We make the sincere wish that others would be freed of this pain, if only we could shoulder that burden on their behalf. That transforms a situation that otherwise would be a big obstacle and another cause of self-pity into something much vaster and an integral component of the path.

There Are Two Tasks, at the Beginning and at the End

The next slogan reads, *There are two tasks, at the beginning and at the end.* Each morning when we wake, we should resolve to turn all actions of body, speech, and mind toward cultivating compassion and bodhichitta. His Holiness the Dalai Lama and many other teachers often recite *The Eight Verses of Mind-Training* in the morning. This short text is about putting oneself low and others high, taking on defeat and giving others the victory, and so forth. Doing this in the morning reminds us what our lives are about. It sets us right for the day. Then, whatever happens during the day, we can recall our aspirations of the morning.

It is also important during our morning practice to set the tone for the day. Here we have another day, another chance to practice. We need to say to ourselves, "During this time I will be careful to keep this awareness, to keep my compassion," and so forth. *The Eight Verses* is a very useful text because there are only eight verses, and they are basically self-explanatory, unlike *The Seven-Point Mind-Training,* which is fairly obscure. The eight verses are simple and quickly said. They set the tone for the day. Therefore, on awakening in the morning, we should resolve to turn all actions of body, speech, and mind toward cultivating compassion and bodhichitta and to be vigilant throughout the day.

That means we have to be careful. We have to be aware. We have to be conscious during the day and not waste time. Whatever actions we are doing, we should try to cultivate mindfulness. We should try to be more conscious. Whomever we meet, we should recognize that they offer an opportunity to be kind and compassionate. They are our helpers on the path. Whether people are nice or mean to us, they can be of help.

Our first thought upon seeing someone is just wishing them well in our heart, recognizing that just as we wish to be happy, all beings wish to be happy, whoever they are. Just like the street dogs here in India: If we pat and speak to them, their tails wag like crazy. They want to be happy. Of course they do—who doesn't? We need to remember that. During the day, whomever we meet, we see them as people who want to be happy, really from our heart. We wish them well. That is part of being vigilant, being conscious during the day and not half-sleepwalking through life.

Just as we want people to be kind and compassionate to us, we also must extend that to others and stop thinking about ourselves so much. To paraphrase Shantideva, if we want to be happy, then we must wish for the happiness of others. If we want to be miserable, we should think only about our own happiness. This is our opportunity.

Then, at the end of the day, we look back on our activities. What have we done with this day, walking on our bodhisattva path? If negative thoughts, speech, or actions have arisen, then we should regret them and determine not to act that way again. It doesn't mean that we flagellate ourselves and get into a spin, angry and upset with ourselves. That is useless, and it just accumulates more negativity. We should, however, sincerely regret our negative actions.

From the heart, we make the commitment that in the future we will be more careful and more conscious. That is how we learn; that is how we begin to grow up and get rid of our childish reactions and responses. That is how we become adults, spiritually speaking. Outwardly we may look like adults, but inwardly many of us still have the emotional responses of four-year-old children.

Then, as we are reflecting on our day, whatever positive things we have done, we rejoice. In Buddhism we regret the negative, but we also rejoice in the positive. Again, while we are pulling out the weeds we also have to pay attention to the good plants. We should not ignore the healthy plants, thinking, "Oh, if I think I did a good thing, that is pride." In fact, we need to appreciate the goodness within us. There is no need to gloat, but we have to encourage ourselves. If we are always focusing on what is wrong with ourselves, then we just end up feeling depressed, with low self-esteem. Self-confidence is essential, as Shantideva says, because we are spiritual warriors.

We have to arouse ourselves to a belief in our innate goodness. Therefore, at the end of the day we regret and determine not to repeat anything negative in body, speech, or mind. If we recognize we have very negative mind patterns, we acknowledge that we are sorry and we try to replace them with positive thoughts. We know that next time we will try to do better. We also recall our positive actions. We humbly rejoice in the good we have done and dedicate any merit to all beings.

We are striving toward goodness for ourselves and so that we have something to contribute to the welfare of the world. The world is very deficient in positive karma at this time, so anything we can do to boost the positive karma levels, we should strive to do. Therefore, we have to remember our goodness and dedicate it to all beings.

Bear Whichever of the Two Occurs

Then the next slogan is, *Bear whichever of the two occurs.* We must make sure that we do not fall prey to the eight worldly concerns. We dealt with this earlier. Gain and loss, praise and blame, good repute and a bad reputation, and pain and pleasure—these opposites bind us in a worldly sense and need to be abandoned. Therefore, we should be careful that whatever actions we undertake do not fall prey to these worldly concerns—about our reputation or about gain and loss, pleasure and pain. Do not let them get caught up in that. We should take fortune and misfortune equally on the path; we should not be swept up when things go absolutely right, just how we want them, or totally cast down when things go wrong.

Here we come back to this idea that everything is dreamlike on one level and the result of karma—all is illusory. It is also impermanent. Now things work well, tomorrow they go wrong, and then they go right again. Impermanence works for us as well as against us; it is not good or bad. It just means things are changing constantly.

If we are going through a bad patch, we can remember that everything is impermanent. We should not grasp at misfortune, because it will change. It is like a wheel, always turning. Sometimes we are up, sometimes we are down. Therefore, if we are only happy when things go right, and completely depressed and stressed out when things go wrong, it is an indication that the real understanding of the Dharma has not entered our hearts.

Even the Buddha got sick, even the Buddha had people throw stones at him, even the Buddha had people criticize him—that is samsara. But how we respond is up to us. When we have understood the Dharma, there should be a certain level of equanimity. We can have an inner equanimity that when things go right, that is nice, and when things go wrong, that is okay also—we will just deal with it.

Whether things go well or whether things go badly, we should have patience, forbearance, tolerance, and equanimity. If we only can practice during good times or only practice during bad times, something is out of balance. A lot of people come to the Dharma because they are suffering. But then, when things start to go well again, they forget all about the Dharma. When things are going well, we tend to get swept away and distracted again by samsara. So, if we can only practice when everything is perfect, or if we are only drawn to the Dharma when things go wrong, then we need to make an adjustment.

When I first became a nun, I went to Thailand. At that time I was twenty-one. I was staying with a friend of mine named John Blofeld, who was a great expert on Chinese Buddhism, although he was very devoted to Tara. He introduced me to a Thai princess, and she took me off to her oceanside estate. I lived in a small but beautiful Thai house made of teak in the middle of a lotus lake, with three servants. Just through the mango groves was a private white sand beach with palm trees and the ocean. I felt very guilty because I thought that I had just renounced the world! So I explained how I felt uncomfortable in all this luxury and indulgence. The princess replied wisely, "Look, you didn't ask for or seek this. It has come to you now. So while it's here, enjoy it. When good things happen, that is nice. But when you leave here, you might be in poverty and difficulties. That's also good. Why are you making this discrimination?"

Sometimes people feel comfortable hanging out in funky places, but if they are in more upbeat, posh surroundings, they feel very uncomfortable. Other people are comfortable in five-star hotels, but if they are in a sleazy motel, they are worrying about all the germs. We need to be equally at home everywhere. Whatever is happening, it is okay. That is the state of mind to cultivate: not to discriminate so much either way. Whatever happens, we accept it and we work with it. It is all fine because that is what is happening in this moment. It is also important for our mind to have equanimity and patience under all circumstances, the good as well as the bad, the bad as well as the good.

Guard the Two at the Cost of Your Life

Guard the two at the cost of your life is the next slogan. The two things that we have to guard, that we must never ever give up, are the precepts and commitments presented in the teachings in general. In other words, refuge in Buddha, Dharma, and Sangha—we never give that up. This includes our commitments in this lojong mind-training, so this means bodhichitta. So the two things that we must never give up are our refuge and bodhichitta. Even at the cost of our lives, we will never abandon the Dharma.

I think Tibetans took this very much to heart during the communist takeover. They never gave up their refuge nor their commitment to bodhichitta, which is why so many lamas, monks, and nuns were imprisoned during those troubled times, and still are to this day. Even at the cost of their lives, they would not even pretend to abandon the Dharma.

Nobody is going to force us to keep this refuge or these precepts, but we see that the Dharma is more important than this particular lifetime. We would never surrender it, for any reason whatsoever. Refuge and bodhichitta both have to be held very closely, held as dearly as our own hearts. No matter how much people offer us, or how much people threaten us, we would never ever abandon our refuge and bodhichitta, from now until enlightenment is reached—not just this lifetime, but all future lifetimes. This is the attitude we cultivate.

Practice the Three Austerities

The next slogan is, *Practice the three austerities.* This is where we have to train. There are three difficulties. First, it is difficult to recognize when afflictive emotions arise. In other words, when we get thoughts of anger or greed or jealousy or just a strong delusory mind with pride and so forth, it is hard for us to recognize that. This is partly because we can coat our negative emotions with some other coloring; we give the emotion nice-sounding names. By the time we have realized that there is anger due to whatever is happening, we have already been carried along.

It is hard to recognize, right in that moment, that this is anger, this is greed. That is why we need to cultivate mindfulness, to become conscious of what thoughts are coming into our mind without justifying them. We need to just see our thoughts and feelings nakedly, recognizing when what is arising is a negative thought, when it is a neutral thought, and even when it is a positive thought.

If we wait until a thought or feeling has gathered force, then we are swept along. It is usually difficult to catch that moment of arising. We tend to be unconscious of what is going on in our minds. Often we are busily cultivating all these negative emotions without even recognizing what is happening inside our mind. The first difficulty therefore is to recognize when these negative thoughts arise in our mind by becoming conscious of all our thoughts.

So now we have recognized our mind state: "I am actually quite angry. I am really irritated by this," or "I really want to reach out and own this desirable object," or whatever. That is the first step. The second difficulty is to turn away from the negative emotion.

However, we might begin to justify this emotion to ourselves with more negative thoughts: "Right now I'm really angry, but I'm justified in being angry. . . ." So we have to develop the ability not only to recognize the negative emotions as they come up, but actually to deal with them skillfully. The one thing that we should *not* do, of course, is just suppress our feelings and pretend they are not there; that just makes them continue to boil inside until they erupt again. The most skillful thing to do after recognizing them is just to accept them and release them. If we can do it, then this would be best. But if we can't, then we try to supply an antidote.

For example, the traditional antidote for feeling angry is to meditate on patience, tolerance, understanding, and compassion. For greed, we meditate on contentment and gratitude. We are always thinking about what we don't have; it is very helpful to appreciate what we actually have—and what more do we really need?

For jealousy, we rejoice in the happiness of others. This is called *mudita*. It's one of the four immeasurable meditations: After loving-kindness and compassion comes the joy in others' pleasure. We develop a real delight that they have got these things. Likewise for any of our negative emotions, there is an antidote. So we should apply that sincerely and watch the negative emotion dissolve.

The third difficulty, alas, is severing the continuity of negative emotions. Even if we have dealt with an unwelcome emotion one day, the next day it comes up again. As we said, dealing with our mental afflictions, or kleshas, is difficult. The word *klesha* has the connotation of something that torments us, something that hurts us like a very hot sun burns the skin.

Normally people are not conscious of how tormented they are by their negativities. Some of us even think they are pleasurable—that is how perverse we are. If we have any of these kleshas arising in the mind, the mind cannot be peaceful. That mind is not calm, and it does not access our wellspring of inner joy. In all Buddhist schools, from the time of the Buddha to the present day, one of the big challenges has been dealing skillfully with the kleshas.

If we think of the diagram of the wheel of life, at the hub in the center are a snake, a pig, and a rooster representing the three poisons. The snake is anger, the rooster is greed, and the pig is delusion, or ignorance. They are biting each other's tails. The whole wheel of samsara keeps turning because of the kleshas.

An arhat, one who has entered nirvana, has completely and utterly uprooted all kleshas, now and forever. An arhat could never be angry, they could never be greedy, and they have no self-delusion. Therefore, they are free. Anyone who demonstrates anger, greed, or delusion is not free; they are still in samsara. Therefore, dealing with the kleshas—transforming them, uprooting them, and finally eradicating them forever—is the primary task in Buddhism.

One of the kleshas is our self-delusion: our belief in a constant, unchanging, permanent "I" at the center of everything. That is the fundamental klesha that gives rise to our greed and grasping and our anger and aversion. All our pleasure and pain, everything, depends on fulfilling the desires of this illusory sense of "I."

Dealing with these kleshas is an important part of severing the continuity. We practice dealing with them in a skillful manner, not by suppressing them, pretending they are not there, or giving in to them, but by transforming and uprooting them from our mind stream. Therefore, Geshe Chekawa advises, in the morning put on the armor. When afflictions arise, recall their antidote. Counter them and resolve that, from now on, you will not allow afflictions to arise in your mind.

Now we come back to the story of the geshe and his piles of white and black stones. The black stones and the white stones were a way for him to be conscious of what was going on in his mind, how much negativity was in his mind, which normally we are not aware of. So this was his skillful method of being alert to what was actually going on in the mind. Gradually he could replace his black pebbles with white pebbles. It wasn't that he was suppressing the black, but he was practicing noticing, and in noticing he could replace that negative thought with a more wholesome thought—a white pebble.

When kleshas arise, Shantideva advises us to face them and question, "Where are its weapons? Where are its muscles? Where is its great army and political strength?" Emotions are just insubstantial thoughts, empty by nature. They come from nowhere, and they remain nowhere. Why, then, are we always overcome by them? They have no strength; they are just empty, vacuous thoughts. Why are we so overcome by them that these emotions can erupt into speech and action?

We should not be afraid: We are much stronger than our kleshas. So in the morning we put on our armor. Our armor is mindfulness and resolve and bodhichitta. Then we can say, "Okay, kleshas, come up and show yourselves. Let's have a look at you. . . . You're pretty puny actually. You think you're important, but you're just thoughts—empty bubbles."

If we really look at our kleshas, they get all shy and try to hide away. They don't want to be looked at because they know if we really face them, they look so stupid. Like those masked Tibetan dancers, they look very powerful with their masks and elaborate costumes on, but when they take all that off, there is only a little monk.

Acquire the Three Principal Causes

Acquire the three principal causes is the next slogan. So these are the three things we need: a qualified master to instruct us, a practice we can commit ourselves to, and sufficient resources that allow us to uphold our practice.

To learn any skill—if we want to be an artist or a musician or an athlete, or even if we want to learn how to use a computer, we need an instructor. We need someone who is more advanced in this skill than we are as a guide. They not only show us how to do things right, but they also can correct our faults so we don't waste time. Otherwise, it is easy to pick up bad habits and, through our ignorance, think they are correct. For example, we might hold our musical instrument the wrong way because it is more comfortable, and we need somebody who knows better to correct us so we can play well.

Of course, in this day and age, it is not so easy to find a qualified lojong teacher, because most of the truly qualified lamas are very busy. They are always running around the world, and if they are well-known enough to find, they have thousands of disciples, so it is hard to cultivate a one-on-one relationship. But nonetheless, when that can happen, it is very useful.

It doesn't mean that we can say, "Oh, you must go to this lama—this is the best lama." That is not true. Some teachers are more helpful for certain people than for others. There is not one teacher who is a Universal Guru. Different people have different connections with different teachers. That is why there is no one teacher in the world whom everybody follows. There couldn't be, because everybody has varied needs and karmic connections.

But it is not so easy nowadays to find a good teacher, one who seems to know us better than we know ourselves and is therefore able to guide us skillfully. It is hard to find one that we can truly trust and to discriminate without being taken in by charisma. In fact, it never has been easy. But if we can find such a one, then that is very important on our spiritual journey.

The second thing we need is a practice we can apply our mind to with faith, enthusiasm, and intelligence. We must have a practice that really speaks to our own heart. This is important, because we have to dedicate ourselves to this practice wholeheartedly. Therefore it has to be the right practice for us.

If we go to a Zen center, there is a Zen meditation. Either it suits us or it doesn't. If we go to a vipashyana center, we are taught vipashyana. We like it or we don't. One of the great things about Tibetan Buddhism is that it has so many skillful means; it has so many different approaches, so many techniques, so many ways to practice. In the beginning this can be confusing. I often say that Tibetan Buddhism is like a Dharma supermarket. We go in, and there are so many items on display. What do we choose? Which is the best?

One time I was in a small supermarket, maybe in California, and there were forty-eight different kinds of yogurt. It wasn't even a big supermarket, just a small shop—with forty-eight different kinds of yogurt! So like that, sometimes Tibetan Buddhism can seem overwhelming. We are spoiled for choice. We don't know which to choose, because like the yogurt each one claims they are the best. There are so many approaches, there are so many practices, and of course each lama will exalt their own tradition. So it is important to find the approach and the technique that speaks to our own heart.

But we are not Tibetans or trying to become Tibetans. I think this is important to remember. Tibetan Buddhism was absolutely perfect for Tibetans, especially living in pre-communist Tibet. But it doesn't mean that everything that was important and meaningful to many medieval Tibetans is necessarily going to be applicable in the twenty-first century, for modern Tibetans or non-Tibetans.

So again this is a challenge: to find a practice that one can take into one's heart and develop that feels meaningful and doesn't go against our modern way of life. We need something that we can take with us and use in our daily life. Because we are not going to be living in medieval Tibet; we are living often in the midst of cities, with families and jobs and relationships.

What practices can we use that will enhance our life as it is right now and not just when we are in retreat?

There isn't any one practice that is absolutely right for everybody, so we have to look for ourselves and find what is really meaningful for us. It needs to be something we can do and carry with us everywhere, so that if we are in New York we are just as much at home practicing as if we were visiting Dharamshala. This is important.

Then our third requirement is relative leisure and the resources to uphold our practice. When we think of it, our needs are actually very simple. We need somewhere to live. We need clothing for our bodies—something for the winter, something for the summer. We need some food that will nourish us and keep us healthy. It is important that we have a certain level of safety and security so that we are able to live and to practice. Beyond that we don't need that much.

In the West, most people could definitely simplify their life, especially if they are somewhere like New York or San Francisco. Instead of applying our energies to earning more so we can buy whatever will keep us up to date with our friends and neighbors, whether a new car or a bigger house or the latest trend in clothes or travel, we could use more of our energies for cultivating our practices and whatever other pursuits we are truly interested in.

Just recently, a friend reminded me about a time when two charming young people came to see me. They were English. One was a teacher of music, and one had a degree in horticulture. Naively, they said, "Is there anything we can do to help you?" As it happened, at the nunnery we were trying to get our landscaping together. So the poor things spent the next few days, even in the rain, trying to replant our gardens and get our landscaping into shape.

The young man, the musician, had been teaching full-time, and after this he drew back a bit and began to work only three days a week. Because he was only working three days a week, he found that, even though he got paid less as a result, his expenses were much less also. He didn't have to pay for transportation backward and forward; he didn't have to buy lunch at work every day. He didn't have all these different expenses that happen when we are working full-time. In fact, for him the financial balance came out equal.

More important, he had so much time left over. He had four days a week during which he wasn't working, so he could do other things and take up other interests. When he tried to persuade his friends—that it worked out the same economically, that he had so much more free time, and that therefore working was also much less stressful—they wouldn't believe him. They couldn't let go of the fact that we have got to keep working, working, working, otherwise our life will fall apart.

It is interesting because we are convinced by our society that we have to be always working, otherwise we will become destitute. While in reality, our basic needs are actually few. If we can find a way to work less and still meet our basic needs, it gives us extra time for doing more meaningful things with less stress. This may not be possible for everyone—often our current financial situation demands that we work not one but two jobs, even—but it is worth asking ourselves the question: "Do I need to work this much? How can I find more time for Dharma practice? What can I change in order to live a less stressful life?"

So we need three things: We need a qualified master, a practice we can apply our mind to, and the relative leisure and resources to uphold our practice.

Cultivate Three Things Without Letting Them Deteriorate

The next slogan is, *Cultivate three things without letting them deteriorate.* There are three things that we must always try to cultivate and develop. The first is undiminished devotion to our master—meaning that if we do have a root guru, we should see them as the Buddha at all times. We should cultivate pure vision toward our teachers and not always be looking for their faults but see that everything they do as a manifestation of pure Buddha activity.

The reasons why masters and devotion to masters are considered important is because of the power of their blessings. The traditional example is that the sun is always shining, but however hot the sun is, if we put a piece of paper on the ground under the sun, the most the sun will do, even after a long time, is make it a bit dry and crackly. But if we hold a magnifying glass between the rays of the sun and the paper, in no time at all it starts to go brown and smoke, and then it bursts into flames. Like the sun's power, the blessings of all the buddhas and bodhisattvas are always around us, but it is hard for us to plug into them. But if we open our hearts to a human teacher, who is a buddha or bodhisattva appearing in human form out of compassion for us, this can quickly open the door to awakening. Our teacher's blessings ignite the fire of our pure insight, and our heart can burst into flames.

Therefore, they are considered the intermediaries between the cosmic buddhas and ourselves, and devotion to them is much easier for us because they are people. That being said, this only works if our devotion is open and pure and basically uncritical. This is the reason why we have to be very careful whom we take as a teacher: If they are a false guru, then the disciple and guru both jump into the chasm. So we have to be sure that they are a qualified teacher.

Then, once one has made that real heart connection, one has to drop one's critical faculties as much as possible—unless the teacher's conduct gets outrageous—and accept their actions as pure buddha activity for our sake. That devotion then gives rise to deep insights and understanding. It is like a corridor with two doors: The guru's door is always open, but if we keep our door closed, then there is no connection. So we have to open our door through devotion to the teacher. Therefore, we cultivate unwavering trust in our master and undiminished joy in bodhichitta and the practice of lojong.

Second, we should take delight in practice. Otherwise, cultivating the lojong attitude such as putting oneself last, thinking of others' happiness and so much about our own happiness and so forth could get to be oppressive. One might assume that hitting away at the self-cherishing mind would reduce all our joy in the world. As stated earlier, if we think, "Oh, it's so hot, I'd like an ice cream—but no! This is just my self-cherishing mind. Just think of all the people in the world with no ice cream," we would feel guilty every time we so much as smile at ourselves! That is not what is intended. Actually, to travel the path, we must have joy.

The Buddha said that even if this Dharma path did involve suffering, it would still be worthwhile because of its fruits. But it is not a path of suffering; it is a path of joy. When people go into retreat and feel that they are putting their whole being into the practice, they seem illumined. It is a great joy, because we are coming back to our source, which is infinite bliss.

Sometimes things are hard. Sometimes obstacles arise. Sometimes our mind is very difficult. Sometimes it is boring and tedious, but ultimately we are chiseling away at the hard rock of our self-cherishing mind, which causes us all our problems. So slowly, slowly, we begin to come back to the real source of our being, which is joyful.

When we talk about emptiness as the nature of the mind, it might sound depressing, but really emptiness just means freedom. It is freedom from grasping. Spaciousness. Openness. Like those gliding eagles just out there in empty spaciousness. They are conscious of what they are doing; they are very alert while they are flying within open spaciousness. That is how our mind should be, like a paraglider in relaxed and effortless poise.

Finally, we also need to have the undiminished wish to help all sentient beings. Down to the smallest insect, we should wish to benefit all living beings and not to harm them in any way. We wish for their well-being: May all beings be well and happy, no exception.

So we have to keep boundless pure intention with us always; we should never allow any of these three things to degenerate. Our devotion, our joy in cultivating bodhichitta in our practice, and our undiminished wish to help all sentient beings—we must ensure they grow more and more as we become acquainted and acclimatized to this way of thinking. It helps to make the mind become vast and all-inclusive.

The word used for mind and heart is the same in Buddhism. The heart/mind becomes wider and wider until it embraces all beings. It is not that I embrace all beings with loving-kindness *except that one*. All beings means *all* beings. This is great freedom.

Maintain Three Things Inseparably

The next slogan is, *Maintain three things inseparably*. This is easy. Make sure our body, speech, and mind, the three inseparable factors, are never separated from virtuous activities. In other words, at all times, under all circumstances, we should try to make sure that our body, speech, and mind are virtuous. We should try to maintain our mindfulness, maintain our bodhichitta, and be alert for kleshas arising in the mind stream. We try to recognize immediately when a thought is negative, when it is not virtuous.

It is a sad reflection on our times that the word *virtue* has become quaint and old-fashioned, but true virtue never goes out of date.

Train Impartially in Every Field

This slogan is not in the root text translation we are using, but it is important. It reads, *Train impartially in every field*. In other words, train wholeheartedly by saturating yourself with this mind-training, this lojong. We must remain resolute in our decisions and train without hesitation. We must also stay single-minded in our practice and not be distracted by other activities. Of course, we have other activities that we give our focused mind to, but the underlying attitude is this practice of lojong—this mind-training of bodhichitta and compassion for others—under all circumstances, no matter what we are doing. We have to blend our mind and heart with the practice so that we become it.

In the Tibetan tradition there are three levels. First, we listen to or study the Dharma. Traditionally in Tibet, people mostly heard discourses—they might not do much reading—so this level simply means to study the Dharma somehow. Next, we think about what we have heard; we investigate and intellectually go over it in the mind so that we really understand it. Last, we meditate and try to incorporate what we have learned into our life. I have also heard it put this way: You hear it, you think about it, then you become it.

With the lojong teachings, we hear them and then we go read books on lojong. This helps us to think about and analyze the subject. Finally, we try to apply these teachings to our lives so eventually we become one with them. This is what we have to do. Then compassion becomes our natural attitude. We are no longer just practicing it; we have become it. Our whole mind is saturated with these ideas—the Dharma and our minds have merged.

It is important that our hearts and the Dharma unite together so we become the Dharma. Usually this happens only through repeated practice. As I said before, it is like a musician or an athlete: For a proficient pianist or a top professional footballer at their peak, their performance seems effortless, as though the music or the sport is playing through them. But this is only because previously they have spent hours, months, and years practicing diligently until they can effortlessly perform. And even then they are still practicing.

I have never met any lama who said, “Okay, I have arrived at my goal, and I am now enlightened!” They always say, “Oh, I’m just like you, I’m still practicing.” Well, they *are* like me, and they are still practicing, but of course they are far ahead and I am still plodding along. The point is that our whole life is a practice, and we never give up until full awakening is attained. In fact, even then we carry on.

The next six slogans are about our orientation toward Dharma practice, toward lojong. They encourage us to be focused, persistent, and consistent and to have trust and conviction in the ability of mind-training to change our minds, change our lives, and lead us toward awakening.

Meditate Constantly on the Distinctive Ones

The next slogan says, *Meditate constantly on the distinctive ones.* This directive advises focusing meditation on specific challenges or situations that provoke strong emotional reactions such as resentment or irritation. This is similar to the slogan from the sixth point: *Whatever mental affliction is strongest, purify that first.* By doing so, practitioners can transform these provocations into opportunities for developing patience, understanding, and deeper compassion.

Do Not Depend on Other Factors

The next slogan is, *Do not depend on other factors.* This slogan encourages maintaining inner stability and commitment to one’s Dharma path regardless of external circumstances. It underscores the importance of not allowing changing situations or conditions to sway our dedication to practice and ethical conduct. It also encourages us to remember to renounce worldly concerns.

Now Practice What Is Important

The next slogan is, *Now practice what is important.* This instruction calls for prioritizing essential aspects of Buddhist practice, which in this case is cultivating bodhichitta—the compassionate mind of enlightenment—and engaging in activities that benefit others. It serves as a reminder to focus on what truly matters for personal and spiritual growth and the well-being of others.

Make No Mistake; Do Not Be Erratic

These two slogans, *Make no mistake* and *Do not be erratic,* highlight the need for consistency and reliability in practice. They caution against vacillation or being unpredictable in one's Dharma commitments, and they advocate for a steady and dependable approach to mind-training and meditation.

Practice with Total Conviction

This exhortation, *Practice with total conviction,* emphasizes engaging in Dharma practice with wholehearted dedication and unwavering confidence. It encourages practitioners to fully commit to their path, embracing the teachings and methods with complete trust and determination.

Free Yourself by Means of Investigation and Analysis

Free yourself by means of investigation and analysis is the next slogan. First of all, we investigate which of the afflictions, which of the kleshas, is most dominant in our mind, and then we apply the appropriate antidote. It is important to work out which of all the many kleshas is rampant in our mind stream—which affliction is the most prominent and the most difficult to deal with. Then we read and study and investigate the antidotes for this, and we become determined to start applying them.

Otherwise, if our knowledge stays only up in the head and doesn't come into our actual actions, then it is not going to help. Merely knowing all the antidotes to anger without applying them is not going to cure anger.

We analyze the ways that our deluded projections arise in relation to specific situations. In other words, if we get angry sometimes, we should analyze which situations or which people bring up that anger in us. Sometimes we are feeling peaceful, then we find ourselves in certain situations or meeting with certain people, and anger arises. So we should look and analyze when that happens.

When we know there are particular situations when we become especially angry, greedy, jealous, or whatever is our particular problem, then we can be on guard. We should be determined to be mindful and careful at those times—to recognize when these kleshas arise and immediately apply the antidote. Once we have recognized what situations press our buttons, we are always ready with the antidote. Otherwise our negative emotions will just carry on, round and round, and we will endlessly blame everybody else for our problems, never recognizing that the real problem is ourselves.

Do Not Try to Make an Impression

The next slogan is, *Do not try to make an impression.* Do not feel too self-congratulatory about your own good deeds or learning or realizations. When we have done some learning and gotten some experiences or realizations in our practice, it should not make us feel proud. Of course, we should appreciate that something is changing inside our mind stream and be happy about that, but it should not make us feel that we are somehow superior to anyone or that this progress makes us special—that attitude is just another klesha. So we should be on guard not to puff ourselves up when something is finally happening in our practice.

Also, we must not expect recognition from others for any kindness we may have done them. Do not expect others to be grateful. We are not working for the sake of others in order to experience their gratitude and appreciation. We don't act in order to get recognition from others for our great good qualities; we just act because that is the right thing to do. Therefore, we shouldn't worry about whether those people are grateful in return. That is totally irrelevant.

If we do a great kindness, and people do not even acknowledge it, we should understand it doesn't matter. We did what we felt was good, and that is enough.

Do Not Be Bound by Distemper

The next slogan reads, *Do not be bound by distemper.* Whatever harmful actions are directed toward us should be ignored, and we should practice patience. Whatever others have done in the past as well, such as humiliating or verbally abusing us, we should let it go. Do not retaliate. Instead, practice these lojong aphorisms, especially in transforming our attitude, and just accept it. It is no big deal.

When people do things that hurt us, harm us, humiliate us, and so forth, these are opportunities to see whether or not we have actually merged our mind with the practice. This is the point Geshe Chekawa is always trying to make: When something goes wrong for us, especially when others hurt us or humiliate us, instead of regarding these people as an obstacle and a problem, we should feel grateful. They are showing us just how much we have understood the practice, how much we have actually merged our mind with the practice.

If we get all hurt and angry and upset, plotting ways to get back at them or thinking of clever things we could have said to completely annihilate them, then this shows we have not understood much. Even then we should feel grateful, because it shows us where we are. Otherwise we cannot know. We often imagine that we are so much nicer than we actually are, or we imagine we are so much worse. It is only when we come to the crunch that we can check how we are doing and whether our practice has seeped down into the heart.

It is like slowly percolating coffee. In Vietnam, when someone makes us coffee in a filter, we sit there and watch it slowly drip. It is slowly percolating down, and the coffee is delicious when we finally get it, but we have to be patient. It is the same with these teachings: They go through all these different levels of the mind until finally the essence percolates down to the heart. We have to be patient, and we have to be persistent. Transformation doesn't happen quickly. Patience and perseverance is the name of the game.

Of course, this does not mean that we should remain passive in an abusive situation or when someone is obviously trying to cheat or harm us. This would be bad karma for them, and they would continue in their negative conduct. But even our show of resistance should be based on compassion rather than anger or fear. The protectors like Mahakala appear very wrathful in order to subdue evil forces, but their motivation is wise compassion. Mahakala is actually the wrathful aspect of Avalokiteshvara, the bodhisattva of compassion.

What the lojong teachings are saying is that when things go wrong and people are mean, instead of feeling upset and angry, we should feel grateful: First, they are giving us a chance to practice; and second, they are showing us where we are really at. Even if we react spontaneously in a negative way, never mind. Now we can see it was a worldly way of reacting, and we know that it is not merging our mind with the lojong practice.

After we have blown it (yet again!), then we can sit quietly and replay the scene from a lojong point of view. In this way we are accustoming our mind to a more skillful response. We can rewrite the script so that our responses are more skillful, more beneficial to ourselves and others. We don't have to repeat the original, traumatic script, which we already know did not help anybody and left us feeling injured inside.

The important thing, therefore, is always to remember that when people push our buttons we should be grateful, because they have made us aware of the buttons we still have—they have illuminated our danger zone. Unless we are conscious of that, we cannot work on it. This is a crucial point.

Do Not Be Temperamental

The next slogan is, *Do not be temperamental.* This means do not indulge in feelings of uncontrollable pleasure or displeasure. Again, if bad things happen, we should not be overly upset or depressed. When good things happen, we should not be overly excited or happy. We remain even-tempered. This doesn't mean that we cannot be happy when good things happen and feel a bit sad when bad things happen—that is being human. It means that we shouldn't cling to those feelings.

We should try to think how to bring our feelings onto the path. Otherwise, we are still caught up in the ocean of samsara, thrown up and pulled down by the waves. Remember the Dharma boat that goes up and down but floats on the waves. Life has ups and downs—there is no avoiding them—so what we need is an aware mind that floats.

We cannot always change outer circumstances, but it is not our outer circumstances that are the problem; it is our inner response that is. The good news is that we can change our inner response, and if we do that, everything changes. If we have an inner equanimity and recognize everything is part of the journey, then there is no problem.

When bad things happen and difficulties arise, some people completely fall to pieces and even magnify the problems in their imagination. Other people just take what is happening as part of the journey and therefore minimize the sense of difficulty. So a lot depends on our inner attitude.

When someone says something negative or critical, some people will feel devastated while other people will just laugh it off. The most significant aspect of what is happening is our response, which is something we can change. This is the whole point of the lojong: Often we cannot change outer circumstances much, but we can use whatever is happening as the actual path.

Even if we never do anything else in this life, we can at least learn how to be the masters of our own minds instead of slaves to it—and if not completely masters, at least semi-masters, subcontractors. That is already a huge step forward.

Do Not Yearn for Gratitude

We have covered the next slogan already: *Do not yearn for gratitude.* If we have been of help to others or have managed to practice for the benefit of others, we should not expect any thanks or praise. We discussed before not expecting recognition from others for our kindness. This is the same idea: We shouldn't expect anyone to be thankful or to praise us for what we do.

The text says if we practice the ultimate and the relative bodhichittas all our life, perform our meditations properly, and mingle our minds with the view, then our experience of daily life will not be ordinary—in other words, ordinary life will become extraordinary. We will genuinely be walking the way of the bodhisattvas. So that is it really. We don't do these things for the sake of winning people's approval.

Concluding Thoughts

Geshe Chekawa says, "Because of my numerous aspirations, I disregarded suffering and censure and sought out the instructions to subdue my ego clinging. Though I may now die, I shall have no regret." For all of us, this is the point. We should live our lives so that whenever we come to die, we can die without regret. We can think: "Well, I made good use of this life. It brought benefit to myself. It brought benefit to others. Fair enough. Now I am ready to go."

The saddest thing is to look back at the end of one's life and recognize that basically we wasted our time on a lot of things that were totally unimportant, and we neglected what really would have helped. So all of us must make the aspiration not to die like that, but to die, even if not yet fully enlightened—I mean, those who can become fully enlightened, good for you—at least feeling that we have walked some little way on the journey, that we didn't waste our precious human birth.

This doesn't mean that we all have to become monks or nuns or hermits and go into lifelong retreat, but it does mean that we should try to merge our lives with the Dharma as much as we can, especially with lojong practices such as bodhichitta and compassion and taking difficulties and challenges as the path.

The beauty of the lojong teachings is that they are so practical. We don't have to be high-level bodhisattvas to follow them. We don't have to spend years and years in intense retreat before we are able to practice. This is a practice for all of us, in accordance with our own capacities. Still, it is a practice that requires us to put the Dharma in the center of our lives; it is not for the periphery when we have enough time. Lojong asks us to make every action a Dharma action—not by changing the action but by changing our attitude. This is wonderful, because outwardly it looks like nothing has changed, but inwardly everything has changed.

Lojong is such a precious teaching because it doesn't require special external circumstances. It doesn't require that we dedicate twelve hours a day to sitting on our cushions. It doesn't require that we lead a monastic life. All it requires is that we really take the teachings on bodhichitta into our lives and use it under all circumstances. Then we will have no regrets.

The universality that makes mind-training such a beautiful teaching is why lojong was taken into all traditions. Apart from the original Kadampa commentaries on lojong, I read Nyingmapa commentaries, Kagyupa commentaries, and Gelugpa commentaries. The Sakyas, of course, also have lojong. Everybody has lojong. And now, it is widely available in books like these, so that everyone can practice it.

Dedicating the Merit

I will now include a beautiful dedication of merit. It is a little long, but please read it now and take its message to heart.

> By this virtue, gathered together with all the merit
> of the ten directions of the three times, buddhas
> and bodhisattvas, saints and sages, realized beings,
> lamas, monks, nuns, yogis, sincere lay practitioners,
> contemplatives of all traditions, and excellent
> practitioners, gathered together with all the
> virtue and good wishes of family, friends, and
> good people everywhere.
>
> By the merit and positive energy of all the good that exists, by the merit of the ultimate nature, by the benefit of beings everywhere effortlessly arising, may all beings benefit. May all beings have happiness and the causes of health and happiness. May all bring healing wherever it

is needed. May this bring about the firm establishment of true health and happiness for us all. May this be the medicine that frees everyone from suffering.

By this merit may all those here and everywhere who are unhappy in any way, confused, angry, afraid, attached, or depressed, with distorted views, be instantly freed from those states. And may they have complete and perfect peace, wisdom, strength, and lasting joy. By the virtue of this practice, by all this merit, may we all be completely free from all the hallucinated afflictive emotions forever. May all those who are suffering from pain or illness immediately be freed from that pain. May they be immediately healed. And may they be firmly established in true and lasting health and happiness.

By this merit, may all those who want to go on retreat find the opportunity to do so very soon. May they all have the resources they need. May they all find suitable conditions. And may their retreat go exceedingly well. And may they have excellent realizations.

By all this merit, may health increase everywhere. May ethics and meditation and wisdom increase. May loving-kindness and compassion increase. And may peace and harmony increase everywhere.

By this merit, may all monasteries, monks, nuns, and lay practitioners, Dharma centers, and social service centers have everything they need to serve people most effectively. And may all their good works flourish.

By this virtue, may we have everything we need to be truly happy. May everything we see, hear, think about, and dream be auspicious.

By this merit, may all the positive, pure wishes we have for each other be completely fulfilled instantly and effortlessly, just as in a Pure Land.

May the pure, supreme jewel, bodhichitta, arise where it has not yet arisen. Where it has arisen, may it not diminish. But may it ever grow and flourish. May warfare cease. May all injury be healed, and all danger pacified. May we produce the conditions for countless generations, starting now, to experience genuine peace. May our intentions equally penetrate every being and place with the true merit of the Buddha's way.

By all this virtue, may all those to whom I am connected by good or bad karma have every happiness. May they all be free from suffering and receive every joy. May they have good health, long life, well-being, strength, comfort, and ease. And may all those who have come to my attention, who have any illness, who are unhappy or in need in any way, be blessed. May they be healed. May they all benefit. May they all have happiness and the causes of health and happiness.

By this virtue, may they all have happiness and the causes of happiness. May those who are in need in any way whatsoever receive every benefit.

By this merit in my mind, may I not withhold any gift whatsoever from any being in any place, wishing them all a great abundance of joys. By all the limitless good that exists, may all the needs of living beings be completely fulfilled.

By all this merit, when this life is over, may we all be reborn immediately in a Pure Land. And in all our lives may we never be separated from qualified teachers and from conducive environments with all the supportive conditions for continuing our practice of the Dharma.

By all this virtue, may I attain complete realization of all practices, and bring all others to that same state. May we all individually attain complete realization of our practice, genuine happiness, health, and peace, wisdom, compassion, and abilities.

By all this merit, may all holy teachers live long and guide us until samsara ends. And may there be peace and joy in all the world.

We dedicate merit because, realistically speaking, if we think we have accumulated this much merit, it is a bit like the water in a mug. When the auspicious circumstances derived from our good karma are finished, the mug is empty. It is like drinking the water. But if we dedicate this virtuous merit by giving and sharing it with all sentient beings, then it is like pouring this water into the ocean. It never diminishes. However much we use it, there is always more. It just increases and increases. This is why it is important to remember to dedicate even a little bit of good karma to all beings: "May this be shared with all beings; may all beings be well and happy." In that way it lightens up the heaviness of our self-seeking desires that so permeate the world at this time. Through dedication, what we have done becomes a virtuous action.

CONCLUSION

The teachings of lojong offer us a profound and transformative opportunity: to bring every aspect of our lives—our joys and sorrows, triumphs and challenges—onto the path of awakening. They invite us to see all experiences, no matter how difficult, as integral parts of our spiritual journey. The essence of these teachings is to welcome life as it is and to train our minds to embrace everything with wisdom and compassion.

When we truly take these teachings to heart, we discover a radical shift in perspective. The difficulties we once saw as obstacles become opportunities for growth. The conflicts that stirred anger now evoke understanding. The sorrows that felt unbearable become gateways to a deeper connection with others. This is the alchemy of mind-training—it transforms adversity into the gold of awakening.

To practice lojong is to live with unwavering courage and boundless compassion. It means meeting our fears, doubts, and challenges with the steadfast resolve to use them as fuel for our practice. It means recognizing that even our habitual tendencies and perceived failures are not signs of weakness but invitations to deepen our understanding of the Dharma. Every moment becomes a chance to cultivate bodhichitta, the awakened heart-mind that seeks the liberation of all beings.

This path asks us to soften where we are rigid, to open where we are closed, and to see the extraordinary potential within the ordinary flow of life. Geshe Chekawa reminds us that everything—every encounter, every emotion, every thought—can serve as a stepping stone toward enlightenment. When we embrace this truth, we unlock the transformative power of the lojong slogans and allow them to illuminate our daily lives.

To integrate these teachings into our lives is an act of courage and devotion. It is a commitment to meet each day with an open heart and a clear mind, to see beyond the illusions of permanence and self, and to embrace the truth of interdependence and emptiness. It is a decision to make compassion our compass and wisdom our guide, weaving the Dharma into the fabric of our existence. This is how we honor the lineage of these teachings and fulfill their ultimate purpose: the liberation of all beings.

Let this not be merely a book we read, but a call to action we heed. May we each take these teachings deeply to heart and dedicate ourselves to living them all. Let us be unafraid to face the full spectrum of human experience and see it all as the path. Whether life brings ease or difficulty, clarity or confusion, let us remember that each moment offers an opportunity to wake up, to open our hearts, and to connect with the vast potential of our buddha nature.

What is the path forward? First, train in the preliminaries and develop the inner attitude that turns toward Dharma and away from nonbeneficial, samsaric things. Second, if you haven't already, take refuge in the Buddha, Dharma, and Sangha and commit to some or all of the five Buddhist precepts. Finally, learn and reflect on the mind-training slogans, so that when adversity arises, you will have the right slogan to apply in that moment.

The path is not always easy, but it is always worth it. May we find the courage to walk it with steadfast determination, the openness to embrace its challenges, and the humility to let its wisdom guide us. May we dedicate ourselves to transforming our lives and the lives of others, one moment, one thought, one breath at a time. And in doing so, may we help bring about a world infused with compassion, wisdom, and boundless love, and joy.

ACKNOWLEDGMENTS

My deepest gratitude to Dr. Pema Düddul for his expertise in combining the two separate commentaries on *The Seven-Point Mind-Training* that I had given some years ago at Deer Park in Himachal Pradesh. It is one thing to give a talk but quite another to render those words into readable text.

I am also indebted to Nikko Odiseos of Shambhala Publications for offering to publish this commentary and to Peter Schumacher for his help in refining the final product. As they explained, there can never be too many books on lojong, especially in this troubled day and age.

Sincere thanks to my ever-resourceful assistant, Felipe Zabala, for liaising with Shambhala and dealing with the protocol while helping to get the manuscript into shape and untie all the various IT knots.

I am always encouraged by the kindness and helpfulness offered by so many people in a process such as this, including the wonderful staff who run Deer Park Institute in Bir, India, and who had invited me to give talks on this *Seven-Point Mind-Training* text.

And of course, heartfelt gratefulness to Geshe Chekawa Yeshe Dorje for providing the original text to be commented on. What a treasure for the world!

INDEX

ABOUT THE AUTHOR

JETSUNMA TENZIN PALMO, born in England in 1943, is a fully ordained nun (*bhikshuni*) in the Drukpa lineage of the Kagyu school of Tibetan Buddhism. She is an author, teacher, and founder of Dongyu Gatsal Ling Nunnery in Himachal Pradesh, India. Jetsunma is renowned for being one of the few Western-born practitioners fully trained in the East, having spent twelve years living in a remote cave in the Himalayas, three of those years in strict meditation retreat. Jetsunma's heart teacher was the Eighth Khamtrul Rinpoche, Dongyu Nyima (1931–1980), who reestablished the Khampagar lineage and monastery in Northern India after the destruction of the original during the Chinese invasion and occupation of Tibet. The title of Jetsunma (revered lady) was bestowed on her by the head of the Drukpa lineage, the Twelfth Gyalwang Drukpa, in recognition of her spiritual achievements as a nun and her efforts in promoting the status of female practitioners in Tibetan Buddhism. No other Westerner has been formally granted a title of such high esteem.